CODECRAFT: A BEGINNER'S GUIDE TO FLUTTER

Dive into Mobile Development with Flutter programming

Francis Mukobi

Table of Contents

FRANKHOST

 FRANCIS MUKOBI

Contents

Preface

Welcome to the world of Flutter! Whether you're new to app development or a seasoned pro, this book is your guide to mastering Flutter and creating stunning native mobile, web, and desktop apps with ease. Flutter's reactive framework and extensive widget library make it a powerful tool for building beautiful, fast apps. In this book, we'll start with the basics and progress to more advanced topics like state management, navigation, and working with APIs. You'll learn how to create custom UIs, handle user input, and integrate Firebase for backend services. Throughout the book, we'll provide practical examples and tips to help you understand Flutter's core concepts and best practices. By the end, you'll have the skills and confidence to create high-quality Flutter apps that stand out in the app stores. Whether you're a beginner or an experienced developer, this book will help you unlock the full potential of Flutter. Let's dive in and start building amazing apps together!

What Flutter is

Flutter is an open-source UI software development kit created by Google. It is used to develop applications for mobile, web, and desktop from a single code base. Flutter allows developers to write code once and deploy it across multiple platforms, making it a powerful tool for building cross-platform applications.

At its core, Flutter uses the Dart programming language, also developed by Google, which provides a fast, object-oriented, and easy-to-learn syntax. Flutter's key feature is its use of widgets, which are the building blocks of the user interface. Widgets in Flutter are highly customizable and can be combined to create complex UIs with smooth animations and transitions.

One of the main advantages of Flutter is its hot reload feature, which allows developers to see changes to their code in real-time, speeding up the development process. Additionally, Flutter provides a rich set of pre-built widgets and libraries that make it easy to create beautiful and responsive applications.

Flutter has gained popularity among developers due to its performance, flexibility, and ease of use. It has been used to build a wide range of applications, from simple mobile apps to complex, high-performance applications used by millions of users.

History and Background of Flutter

Flutter, Google's open-source UI software development kit, was first unveiled at the Dart Developer Summit in 2015 under the name "Sky." It was initially designed as a framework for creating high-performance, animated apps for iOS and Android from a single codebase. The project was later renamed to Flutter and made public during the Google I/O conference in 2017.

The primary goal behind Flutter's development was to address the challenges faced by mobile app developers, such as the need to write separate codebases for iOS and Android, as well as the lack of a consistent and expressive UI framework. Flutter aimed to provide a solution that would allow developers to write code once and deploy it across multiple platforms without compromising on performance or user experience.

One of the key technologies behind Flutter is the Dart programming language. Dart was also developed by Google and was designed with the goal of being fast, object-oriented, and easy to learn. Flutter uses Dart to provide a reactive framework that enables the creation of highly customizable and performant user interfaces.

Since its initial release, Flutter has undergone significant development and has gained popularity among developers worldwide. It has been used to build a wide range of applications, from simple prototypes to complex, production-ready apps used by millions of users. Flutter's growing community of developers, along with its rich set of features and tools, has solidified its position as a leading framework for cross-platform app development.

In addition to mobile apps, Flutter has expanded its reach to other platforms, including web and desktop. Google continues to invest in

Flutter's development, with regular updates and new features being added to the framework to further enhance its capabilities and usability.

Features and Advantages of Flutter

Flutter, Google's UI toolkit for building natively compiled applications for mobile, web, and desktop from a single codebase, offers a wide range of features and advantages that make it a popular choice among developers. Here's a comprehensive overview of Flutter's key features and advantages:

1. Hot Reload:

- One of Flutter's most notable features is its hot reload capability, which allows developers to make changes to their code and see the results instantly without restarting the app. This feature significantly speeds up the development process and allows for quick experimentation and iteration.

2. Single Codebase:

- With Flutter, developers can write code once and deploy it across multiple platforms, including iOS, Android, web, and desktop. This reduces development time and effort, as developers don't need to maintain separate codebases for each platform.

3. Expressive UI Framework:

- Flutter provides a rich set of customizable widgets that allow developers to create beautiful and highly responsive user interfaces. These widgets are designed to adapt to different screen sizes and pixel densities, ensuring a consistent user experience across devices.

4. Fast Performance:

- Flutter apps are compiled directly to native machine code, which results in high performance and smooth animations. Flutter's reactive framework also minimizes the need for constant redraws, leading to faster rendering times.

5. Access to Native Features:

- Flutter provides access to a wide range of native features and APIs, allowing developers to integrate platform-specific functionality into their apps. This includes camera, geolocation, sensors, and more.

6. Rich Set of Libraries and Packages:

- Flutter has a vibrant ecosystem of libraries and packages that provide additional functionality and make common tasks easier. This includes packages for state management, networking, navigation, and more.

7. Strong Community Support:

- Flutter has a large and active community of developers who contribute to its development and provide support through forums, tutorials, and open-source projects. This community-driven approach ensures that Flutter remains up-to-date and well-supported.

8. Cross-Platform Development:

- Flutter's cross-platform nature allows developers to build apps that run seamlessly on multiple platforms, reducing development time and costs. This makes it an ideal choice for businesses looking to reach a wider audience with their apps.

9. Integration with Firebase:

- Flutter integrates seamlessly with Firebase, Google's mobile platform that provides a suite of backend services for building apps. This allows developers to easily add features such as authentication, analytics, and cloud storage to their Flutter apps.

10. Growing Popularity and Adoption:

- Flutter has gained significant popularity and adoption since its release, with many companies and developers choosing it for their app development needs. This widespread adoption is a testament to Flutter's capabilities and the benefits it offers to developers.

In conclusion, Flutter's features and advantages make it a powerful and versatile framework for building cross-platform applications. Its ease of use, fast performance, expressive UI framework, and strong community support make it an attractive choice for developers looking to create high-quality apps for a variety of platforms.

Getting Started with Flutter

To get started with Flutter, follow these steps:

1. Install Flutter:

- Download the Flutter SDK from the official website (https://flutter.dev/docs/get-started/install) and follow the installation instructions for your operating system.

2. Set Up Your IDE:

- Install and set up an IDE (Integrated Development Environment) for Flutter development. Popular choices include Android Studio, Visual Studio Code, and IntelliJ IDEA. Install the Flutter and Dart plugins/extensions for your chosen IDE.

3. Create a New Flutter Project:

- Use the Flutter CLI (Command Line Interface) to create a new Flutter project. Open a terminal and run the following command:

```lua
flutter create my_flutter_app
```

- Replace my_flutter_app with the name of your project.

4. Run Your Flutter App:

- Navigate to your project directory in the terminal and run your Flutter app on a connected device or emulator:

```arduino
cd my_flutter_app
flutter run
```

5. Explore Flutter Widgets:

- Flutter uses widgets to create user interfaces. Explore the different types of widgets available in Flutter, such as Container, Row, Column, Text, Image, and more. Modify the default Flutter app code to experiment with these widgets and see how they affect the UI.

6. Learn Dart Programming:

- Flutter uses the Dart programming language. Familiarize yourself with Dart syntax, features, and concepts such as classes, functions, variables, and data types. Dart's official website (https://dart.dev/) provides comprehensive documentation and resources for learning Dart.

7. Customize Your App:

- Modify the default Flutter app code to customize the appearance and behavior of your app. Experiment with different widgets, layouts, colors, fonts, and styles to create a unique user interface.

8. Add Functionality:

- Implement functionality in your Flutter app, such as handling user input, navigation between screens, and fetching data from APIs. Use Flutter plugins to access native device features and services.

9. Test Your App:

- Test your Flutter app on different devices and screen sizes to ensure compatibility and responsiveness. Use Flutter's debugging tools to identify and fix any issues in your code.

10. Publish Your App:

- Once your Flutter app is ready, you can publish it to the Google Play Store for Android apps and the Apple App Store for iOS apps. Follow the respective app store guidelines and requirements for publishing your app.

Getting started with Flutter is an exciting journey into the world of cross-platform app development. Experiment, explore, and have fun building beautiful and functional apps with Flutter!

Getting Started with Flutter: A Comprehensive Guide for Beginners

Flutter is Google's open-source UI software development kit that enables developers to create natively compiled applications for mobile, web, and desktop from a single codebase. Whether you're new to mobile app development or looking to expand your skill set, getting started with Flutter is an exciting journey. This comprehensive guide will walk you through the process of setting up your development environment, creating your first Flutter project, and building a simple app.

1. Install Flutter:

- Start by downloading the Flutter SDK from the official Flutter website (https://flutter.dev/docs/get-started/install) and follow the installation instructions for your operating system.

2. Set Up Your IDE:

- Flutter supports various IDEs, including Android Studio, Visual Studio Code, and IntelliJ IDEA. Install your preferred IDE and add the Flutter and Dart plugins/extensions for seamless Flutter development.

3. Create a New Flutter Project:

- Use the Flutter CLI (Command Line Interface) to create a new Flutter project. Open a terminal and run the following command:

lua code
flutter create my_flutter_app

- Replace my_flutter_app with the name of your project.

4. Run Your Flutter App:

- Navigate to your project directory in the terminal and run your Flutter app on a connected device or emulator:

arduino code
cd my_flutter_app
flutter run

5. Learn Flutter Basics:

- Familiarize yourself with Flutter's basic concepts, such as widgets, layouts, and state management. Flutter uses a reactive framework, where widgets are the building blocks of the user interface.

6. Customize Your App:

- Modify the default Flutter app code to customize the appearance and behavior of your app. Experiment with different widgets, colors, fonts, and layouts to create a unique user interface.

7. Add Functionality:

- Implement functionality in your Flutter app, such as handling user input, navigating between screens, and fetching data from APIs. Use Flutter plugins to access device features and services.

8. Test Your App:

- Test your Flutter app on different devices and screen sizes to ensure compatibility and responsiveness. Use Flutter's debugging tools to identify and fix any issues in your code.

9. Publish Your App:

- Once your Flutter app is ready, you can publish it to the Google Play Store for Android apps and the Apple App Store for iOS apps. Follow the respective app store guidelines and requirements for publishing your app.

10. Continue Learning:

- Flutter offers a wealth of resources, including documentation, tutorials, and community forums. Continuously improve your Flutter skills by exploring advanced topics and staying updated with the latest Flutter developments.

Getting started with Flutter is an exciting and rewarding experience. With Flutter's rich set of features and vibrant community, you'll be on your way to building beautiful and functional apps in no time.

Getting Started with Flutter: A Comprehensive Guide

Flutter is an open-source UI software development kit created by Google, designed to help developers build natively compiled applications for mobile, web, and desktop from a single codebase. If you're new to Flutter and looking to get started, this guide will walk you through the essential steps to set up your development environment, create your first Flutter project, and build a basic app.

1. Install Flutter:

- Start by downloading the Flutter SDK from the official Flutter website (https://flutter.dev/docs/get-started/install) and follow the installation instructions for your operating system.

2. Set Up Your IDE:

- Flutter is compatible with various Integrated Development Environments (IDEs) such as Android Studio, Visual Studio Code, and IntelliJ IDEA. Install your preferred IDE and add the Flutter and Dart plugins/extensions for seamless Flutter development.

3. Create a New Flutter Project:

- Use the Flutter CLI (Command Line Interface) to create a new Flutter project. Open a terminal and run the following command:

lua code
flutter create my_first_flutter_app

- Replace my_first_flutter_app with the desired name of your project.

4. Run Your Flutter App:

- Navigate to your project directory in the terminal and run your Flutter app on a connected device or emulator:

arduino code
cd my_first_flutter_app
flutter run

5. Learn Flutter Basics:

- Familiarize yourself with Flutter's basic concepts, such as widgets, layouts, and state management. Flutter uses a reactive framework, where widgets are the building blocks of the user interface.

6. Customize Your App:

- Modify the default Flutter app code to customize the appearance and behavior of your app. Experiment with different widgets, colors, fonts, and layouts to create a unique user interface.

7. Add Functionality:

- Implement functionality in your Flutter app, such as handling user input, navigating between screens, and fetching data from APIs. Use Flutter plugins to access device features and services.

8. Test Your App:

- Test your Flutter app on different devices and screen sizes to ensure compatibility and responsiveness. Use Flutter's debugging tools to identify and fix any issues in your code.

9. Publish Your App:

- Once your Flutter app is ready, you can publish it to the Google Play Store for Android apps and the Apple App Store for iOS apps. Follow the respective app store guidelines and requirements for publishing your app.

10. Continue Learning:

- Flutter offers a wealth of resources, including documentation, tutorials, and community forums. Continuously improve your Flutter skills by exploring advanced topics and staying updated with the latest Flutter developments.

Getting started with Flutter is an exciting journey that opens up a world of possibilities for app development. By following this guide, you'll be well on your way to creating beautiful and functional apps with Flutter.

Installing Flutter SDK

To install the Flutter SDK, follow these steps:

1. **Download Flutter:**
   - Visit the Flutter website at https://flutter.dev/docs/get-started/install and download the Flutter SDK for your operating system (Windows, macOS, Linux).
2. **Extract the ZIP File:**
   - Once the download is complete, extract the contents of the ZIP file to a location on your computer.
3. **Set Up Environment Variables (Windows):**
   - If you're using Windows, you'll need to add the Flutter bin directory to your system's PATH environment variable. This allows you to run Flutter commands from the command line.
     - Open the Control Panel and go to System and Security > System > Advanced system settings.
     - Click on Environment Variables, then under System Variables, find the PATH variable and click Edit.
     - Add the full path to the Flutter bin directory (e.g., C:\src\flutter\bin) to the list of paths and click OK.
4. **Set Up Environment Variables (macOS/Linux):**
   - If you're using macOS or Linux, you can add the Flutter bin directory to your PATH by editing the

.bashrc or .zshrc file in your home directory and adding the following line:

```bash
bash code
export PATH="$PATH:/path/to/flutter/bin"
```

- Replace /path/to/flutter/bin with the actual path to your Flutter bin directory.

1. **Verify Installation:**
   - Open a new terminal window and run the following command to verify that Flutter is installed correctly:

```css
css code
flutter—version
```

- You should see the Flutter version information printed to the console.

1. **Run Flutter Doctor:**
   - Run the following command to check if there are any dependencies you need to install to complete the Flutter setup:

```
code
flutter doctor
```

- Follow the instructions printed by the Flutter doctor to install any missing dependencies.

1. **Update Flutter:**
   - Periodically, you may want to update your Flutter installation to get the latest features and bug fixes. You can do this by running the following command:

```
code
flutter upgrade
```

Once you have completed these steps, you will have successfully installed the Flutter SDK on your computer. You can now start developing Flutter apps using your favorite code editor or IDE.

Setting up IDE (Android Studio, Visual Studio Code)

To set up your IDE (Integrated Development Environment) for Flutter development, follow these steps for Android Studio and Visual Studio Code:

Setting up Android Studio:

1. **Install Android Studio:**
   - Download and install Android Studio from the official website: https://developer.android.com/studio

2. **Install Flutter and Dart Plugins:**
   - Open Android Studio and go to File > Settings (or Android Studio > Preferences on macOS).
   - In the Settings/Preferences dialog, select Plugins on the left.
   - Click on the Marketplace tab and search for "Flutter."
   - Click the Install button next to the Flutter plugin.
   - Repeat the same process for the Dart plugin.

3. **Set Flutter SDK Path:**
   - Go to File > Settings (or Android Studio > Preferences on macOS).
   - In the Settings/Preferences dialog, select Languages & Frameworks > Flutter.
   - Set the Flutter SDK path to the directory where you installed Flutter.

4. **Create a New Flutter Project:**

- Click on File > New > New Flutter Project.
- Follow the prompts to create a new Flutter project.

5. **Run Your Flutter App:**
    - Connect a device or start an emulator.
    - Click on the Run icon in the toolbar, or select Run > Run 'main.dart' from the menu.

Setting up Visual Studio Code:

1. **Install Visual Studio Code:**
    - Download and install Visual Studio Code from the official website: https://code.visualstudio.com/

2. **Install Flutter and Dart Extensions:**
    - Open Visual Studio Code and go to the Extensions view by clicking on the square icon in the sidebar or by pressing Ctrl+Shift+X.
    - Search for "Flutter" and "Dart" extensions.
    - Click the Install button for each extension.

3. **Set Flutter SDK Path:**
    - Open the Command Palette by pressing Ctrl+Shift+P (or Cmd+Shift+P on macOS).
    - Search for "Flutter: Change SDK" and select it.
    - Enter the path to your Flutter SDK directory.

4. **Create a New Flutter Project:**
    - Open the Command Palette (Ctrl+Shift+P or Cmd+Shift+P) and search for "Flutter: New Project."
    - Follow the prompts to create a new Flutter project.

5. **Run Your Flutter App:**
    - Open the main.dart file in your Flutter project.
    - Click on the Run icon in the toolbar, or press F5 to start debugging.

With these steps, you should have Android Studio or Visual Studio Code set up for Flutter development. You can now start coding your Flutter apps using your preferred IDE.

Creating Your First Flutter Project

To create your first Flutter project, follow these steps:

1. **Install Flutter:**
    - Download and install the Flutter SDK from the official website: flutter.dev
2. **Set Up Your Development Environment:**
    - Follow the installation instructions for your operating system to set up Flutter and configure your development environment.
3. **Create a New Flutter Project:**
    - Open a terminal or command prompt.
    - Use the following command to create a new Flutter project:

lua code
```lua
flutter create my_first_flutter_project
```

- Replace my_first_flutter_project with the name of your project.

1. **Run Your Flutter App:**
    - Navigate to your project directory:

bash code
```bash
cd my_first_flutter_project
```

- Run your Flutter app on a connected device or emulator:

arduino code

flutter run

1. **Explore Your Flutter Project:**
    ◦ Open the project in your preferred IDE (such as Android Studio or Visual Studio Code).
    ◦ Explore the project structure and files, including the lib directory where your Dart code is located.
2. **Modify Your App:**
    ◦ Open the lib/main.dart file in your IDE.
    ◦ Make changes to the default app code to customize your app's appearance and behavior.
3. **Hot Reload:**
    ◦ Use the hot reload feature to see your changes instantly reflected in the running app:
        ▪ Make a change in your code.
        ▪ Save the file (Ctrl+S or Cmd+S).
        ▪ See the changes immediately in the running app without restarting it.
4. **Learn Flutter Widgets:**
    ◦ Familiarize yourself with Flutter's widgets, which are the building blocks of Flutter apps. Experiment with different widgets to create your app's user interface.
5. **Continue Learning:**
    ◦ Explore the Flutter documentation and tutorials to learn more about Flutter development and best practices.
6. **Celebrate Your First Flutter Project:**
    ◦ Congratulations! You've created your first Flutter project. Keep building and experimenting with Flutter to create amazing apps.

Understanding Widgets

In Flutter, everything is a widget. Widgets are the building blocks of Flutter apps, used to create the user interface and define the layout and behavior of the app's UI elements. Understanding widgets is essential for developing Flutter apps effectively. Here's a comprehensive overview of widgets in Flutter:

1. What is a Widget?

- A widget is a lightweight, immutable description of part of a user interface. Widgets can be as simple as a button or as complex as a full-screen layout.

2. Types of Widgets:

- **StatelessWidget:** Represents a widget that does not require mutable state. Stateless widgets are immutable, meaning their properties cannot change once they are initialized.
- **StatefulWidget:** Represents a widget that can maintain mutable state. Stateful widgets are dynamic and can change their appearance in response to user interactions or other events.

3. Widget Composition:

- Flutter uses a composition model, where complex widgets are built by combining simpler widgets. This allows for the creation of rich and flexible UIs.

4. Common Widgets:

- **Container:** A widget that allows you to create a rectangular visual element. It can be styled using properties such as color, border, and padding.
- **Row and Column:** Widgets that arrange their children in a horizontal (Row) or vertical (Column) line.
- **Text:** A widget that displays a text string with optional styling.
- **Image:** A widget that displays an image from various sources, such as the network or local storage.
- **ListView:** A scrollable list of widgets arranged linearly.
- **GestureDetector:** A widget that detects gestures, such as taps, swipes, and drags, allowing for interactive elements in the app.

5. Widget Lifecycle:

- Stateful widgets have a lifecycle that includes the following methods:
    - **initState():** Called when the widget is first inserted into the tree.
    - **didChangeDependencies():** Called when the widget's dependencies change.
    - **build():** Called to build the widget's UI.
    - **didUpdateWidget():** Called when the widget is rebuilt with different properties.
    - **dispose():** Called when the widget is removed from the tree.

6. Widget Rebuilding:

- Flutter uses a reactive framework, meaning widgets can rebuild in response to changes in their state or properties. This allows for dynamic and responsive UIs.

7. Widget Tree:

- Widgets are organized in a tree structure, with each widget containing its own subtree of child widgets. This allows for the creation of complex UIs by nesting widgets within each other.

Understanding widgets is fundamental to developing Flutter apps. By mastering the concept of widgets and how they work together, you can create beautiful and responsive user interfaces for your Flutter apps.

Stateful vs. Stateless Widgets

Stateless Widgets:
Stateless widgets are immutable widgets that do not require mutable state. Once a stateless widget is created, its properties cannot change. Stateless widgets are simple and efficient, making them ideal for UI elements that do not change based on user interactions or other factors.

Example of a stateless widget:

```dart
dart code
class MyStatelessWidget extends StatelessWidget {
@override
Widget build(BuildContext context) {
return Container(
color: Colors.blue,
child: Text('Hello, World!'),
);
}
}
```

Stateful Widgets:
Stateful widgets, on the other hand, can maintain mutable state. They are dynamic and can change their appearance in response to user interactions or other events. Stateful widgets are more complex than stateless widgets but are necessary for building interactive UIs.

Example of a stateful widget:

```dart
dart code
class MyStatefulWidget extends StatefulWidget {
@override
_MyStatefulWidgetState createState() => _MyStatefulWidgetState();
}
class _MyStatefulWidgetState extends State<MyStatefulWidget> {
bool _isButtonPressed = false;
```

```
@override
Widget build(BuildContext context) {
return RaisedButton(
onPressed: () {
setState(() {
_isButtonPressed = !_isButtonPressed;
});
},
child: Text(_isButtonPressed ? 'Pressed' : 'Not Pressed'),
);
}
}
```

In the above example, _MyStatefulWidgetState is a state class that extends State<MyStatefulWidget>. The _isButtonPressed variable is mutable state that determines the text displayed on the button. When the button is pressed, the setState method is called to update the state and trigger a rebuild of the widget.

Choosing Between Stateless and Stateful Widgets:

- Use stateless widgets for static UI elements that do not change.
- Use stateful widgets for dynamic UI elements that change based on user interactions or other factors.

Understanding the difference between stateless and stateful widgets is crucial for developing Flutter apps, as it determines how you manage and update your app's UI based on its state.

Layouts and Widgets

In Flutter, layouts are created using widgets to arrange and display UI elements. Widgets are the building blocks of Flutter applications, and each widget serves a specific purpose in defining the UI. Understanding layouts and widgets is essential for creating well-structured and visually appealing Flutter apps. Here's an overview of common layouts and widgets used in Flutter:

1. Layout Widgets:

- **Container:** A widget that allows you to create a rectangular visual element with optional styling properties such as color, border, padding, and margin.
- **Row and Column:** Widgets used to arrange their children in a horizontal (Row) or vertical (Column) line. These widgets are essential for creating flexible and responsive layouts.
- **Stack:** A widget that allows you to stack children on top of each other. Useful for creating overlapping UI elements.
- **ListView:** A scrollable list of widgets arranged linearly. Allows you to display a large number of items efficiently.
- **GridView:** A scrollable grid of widgets. Useful for displaying items in a grid layout, such as a photo gallery or a product catalog.
- **Expanded:** A widget that expands its child to fill the available space. Used within Row, Column, or Flex widgets to control the layout's flexibility.

2. Common Widgets:

- **Text:** A widget that displays a text string with optional styling properties such as font size, color, and alignment.

- **Image:** A widget that displays an image from various sources, such as the network, local storage, or assets.
- **Icon:** A widget that displays a material design icon. Icons can be customized with size, color, and alignment properties.
- **Button Widgets (FlatButton, RaisedButton, IconButton):** Widgets that represent interactive elements that users can tap or click. Each button widget has its own style and behavior.
- **TextField:** A widget that allows users to input text. TextField widgets can be customized with various properties, such as placeholder text, input validation, and input formatting.

3. Using Layout Widgets:

- To create a layout in Flutter, you typically start with a top-level layout widget, such as MaterialApp, Scaffold, or Container.
- Use nested layout widgets, such as Row, Column, Stack, and ListView, to arrange child widgets within the parent widget.
- Customize the appearance of widgets using properties and parameters specific to each widget. For example, you can set the color, size, and alignment of a widget using its properties.
- Use Flutter's hot reload feature to quickly see the effects of your changes and iterate on your layout design.

4. Best Practices:

- Keep layouts simple and avoid nesting too many widgets. Use layout widgets like Row, Column, and Flex to create flexible and responsive designs.
- Use Flutter's widget composition model to build complex UIs by combining simple widgets.

- Use Flutter's MediaQuery and LayoutBuilder widgets to create responsive layouts that adapt to different screen sizes and orientations.

By understanding layouts and widgets in Flutter, you can create visually appealing and responsive UIs for your Flutter applications. Experiment with different layouts and widgets to create unique and engaging user experiences.

Layouts and Widgets

In Flutter, layouts are created using widgets to arrange and display UI elements. Widgets are the building blocks of Flutter applications, and each widget serves a specific purpose in defining the UI. Understanding layouts and widgets is essential for creating well-structured and visually appealing Flutter apps. Here's an overview of common layouts and widgets used in Flutter:

1. Layout Widgets:

- **Container:** A widget that allows you to create a rectangular visual element with optional styling properties such as color, border, padding, and margin.
- **Row and Column:** Widgets used to arrange their children in a horizontal (Row) or vertical (Column) line. These widgets are essential for creating flexible and responsive layouts.
- **Stack:** A widget that allows you to stack children on top of each other. Useful for creating overlapping UI elements.
- **ListView:** A scrollable list of widgets arranged linearly. Allows you to display a large number of items efficiently.
- **GridView:** A scrollable grid of widgets. Useful for displaying items in a grid layout, such as a photo gallery or a product catalog.
- **Expanded:** A widget that expands its child to fill the available space. Used within Row, Column, or Flex widgets to control the layout's flexibility.

2. Common Widgets:

- **Text:** A widget that displays a text string with optional

styling properties such as font size, color, and alignment.
- **Image:** A widget that displays an image from various sources, such as the network, local storage, or assets.
- **Icon:** A widget that displays a material design icon. Icons can be customized with size, color, and alignment properties.
- **Button Widgets (FlatButton, RaisedButton, IconButton):** Widgets that represent interactive elements that users can tap or click. Each button widget has its own style and behavior.
- **TextField:** A widget that allows users to input text. TextField widgets can be customized with various properties, such as placeholder text, input validation, and input formatting.

3. Using Layout Widgets:

- To create a layout in Flutter, you typically start with a top-level layout widget, such as MaterialApp, Scaffold, or Container.
- Use nested layout widgets, such as Row, Column, Stack, and ListView, to arrange child widgets within the parent widget.
- Customize the appearance of widgets using properties and parameters specific to each widget. For example, you can set the color, size, and alignment of a widget using its properties.
- Use Flutter's hot reload feature to quickly see the effects of your changes and iterate on your layout design.

4. Best Practices:

- Keep layouts simple and avoid nesting too many widgets. Use layout widgets like Row, Column, and Flex to create flexible and responsive designs.
- Use Flutter's widget composition model to build complex UIs by combining simple widgets.

- Use Flutter's MediaQuery and LayoutBuilder widgets to create responsive layouts that adapt to different screen sizes and orientations.

By understanding layouts and widgets in Flutter, you can create visually appealing and responsive UIs for your Flutter applications. Experiment with different layouts and widgets to create unique and engaging user experiences.

Handling User input

Handling user input is a crucial aspect of developing interactive Flutter applications. Flutter provides various widgets and mechanisms to handle user interactions such as taps, gestures, text input, and more. Here's an overview of how you can handle user input in Flutter:

1. GestureDetector Widget:

- The GestureDetector widget is used to detect gestures such as taps, drags, and long presses. You can wrap any widget with a GestureDetector to make it interactive.

```dart
dart code
GestureDetector(
onTap: () {
// Handle tap event
},
child: Container(
width: 100,
height: 100,
color: Colors.blue,
child: Center(child: Text('Tap me')),
),
)
```

2. InkWell Widget:

- The InkWell widget is a material widget that responds to touches. It provides a visual ripple effect when tapped and can be used to make any widget interactive.

```dart
dart code
```

```
InkWell(
onTap: () {
// Handle tap event
},
child: Container(
width: 100,
height: 100,
color: Colors.blue,
child: Center(child: Text('Tap me')),
),
)
```

3. TextField Widget:

- The TextField widget is used to accept text input from the user. You can use the onChanged callback to listen for changes to the text input.

```
dart code
TextField(
onChanged: (text) {
// Handle text input
},
decoration: InputDecoration(
labelText: 'Enter your name',
),
)
```

4. GestureDetector for Tap Handling:

- You can use the GestureDetector widget to handle taps on any widget.

```
dart code
GestureDetector(
onTap: () {
// Handle tap event
},
child: Container(
```

```
width: 100,
height: 100,
color: Colors.blue,
child: Center(child: Text('Tap me')),
),
)
```

5. GestureRecognizer for Complex Gestures:

- For more complex gestures, you can use the GestureRecognizer class to create custom gesture recognizers.

```dart
dart code
GestureDetector(
onPanUpdate: (details) {
// Handle pan update event
},
child: Container(
width: 100,
height: 100,
color: Colors.blue,
child: Center(child: Text('Drag me')),
),
)
```

6. Handling Form Submission:

- To handle form submissions, you can use the Form widget along with TextFormField widgets for text input.

```dart
dart code
Form(
child: Column(
children: [
TextFormField(
// Form field for name input
),
RaisedButton(
onPressed: () {
```

```
// Handle form submission
},
child: Text('Submit'),
),
],
),
)
```

7. Using TextEditingController:

- You can use the TextEditingController class to control the text entered in a TextField widget and listen for changes to the text input.

```dart
dart code
final TextEditingController _controller = TextEditingController();
TextField(
controller: _controller,
onChanged: (text) {
// Handle text input
},
)
```

These are some common ways to handle user input in Flutter. By using these widgets and techniques, you can create interactive and user-friendly Flutter applications.

Navigation and Routing

Navigation and routing are essential concepts in Flutter for moving between different screens or pages within an app. Flutter provides a flexible and powerful navigation system that allows you to manage app navigation efficiently. Here's an overview of how navigation and routing work in Flutter:

1. Navigator Class:

- The Navigator class manages a stack of Route objects and is used to navigate between different screens in a Flutter app.

```dart
dart code
Navigator.push(
context,
MaterialPageRoute(builder: (context) => SecondScreen()),
);
```

2. MaterialPageRoute Class:

- The MaterialPageRoute class is used to define a route that displays a fullscreen modal dialog.

```dart
dart code
MaterialPageRoute(builder: (context) => SecondScreen())
```

3. Navigator.pop():

- The Navigator.pop() method is used to close the current screen and return to the previous screen.

```dart
dart code
Navigator.pop(context);
```

4. Named Routes:

- Named routes allow you to define routes with names, making it easier to navigate between screens.

```dart
dart code
MaterialApp(
routes: {
'/': (context) => HomeScreen(),
'/second': (context) => SecondScreen(),
},
)
```

5. Navigate to Named Routes:

- You can use the named routes defined in the MaterialApp to navigate to a specific screen.

```dart
dart code
Navigator.pushNamed(context, '/second');
```

6. Passing Data Between Screens:

- You can pass data between screens using the arguments parameter of MaterialPageRoute or by using a state management solution like Provider or Riverpod.

```dart
dart code
Navigator.push(
context,
MaterialPageRoute(
builder: (context) => SecondScreen(data: 'Hello'),
),
);
```

7. Using onGenerateRoute:

- The onGenerateRoute property of MaterialApp can be used to define a function that generates routes dynamically.

```dart
dart code
```

```dart
MaterialApp(
onGenerateRoute: (settings) {
if (settings.name == '/second') {
return MaterialPageRoute(
builder: (context) => SecondScreen(),
);
}
// Handle other routes
},
)
```

8. NavigatorObservers:

- NavigatorObservers can be used to listen to navigation events and perform actions based on those events.

```dart
dart code
class MyNavigatorObserver extends NavigatorObserver {
@override
void didPush(Route<dynamic> route, Route<dynamic>? previousRoute) {
// Handle navigation events
}
}
```

9. Using BottomNavigationBar and TabBarView:

- BottomNavigationBar and TabBarView widgets can be used to create apps with bottom navigation or tabbed navigation.

```dart
dart code
BottomNavigationBar(
items: [
BottomNavigationBarItem(
icon: Icon(Icons.home),
label: 'Home',
),
BottomNavigationBarItem(
icon: Icon(Icons.settings),
label: 'Settings',
```

```
),
],
onTap: (index) {
// Handle navigation based on index
},
)
```

Flutter's navigation and routing system provides a flexible and intuitive way to manage app navigation. By using these concepts and widgets, you can create smooth and seamless navigation experiences in your Flutter apps.

Flutter UI Design:

Styling Your App:

- Flutter allows you to style your app using the built-in Material Design or Cupertino (iOS-style) themes, or by customizing the style of individual widgets.
- You can use properties like color, fontSize, fontWeight, and decoration to style widgets such as Text, Container, and AppBar.
- Flutter's Theme widget allows you to define a theme for your entire app, making it easy to maintain a consistent look and feel.

Working with Themes:

- Themes in Flutter are used to define the overall look and feel of your app, including colors, typography, and shapes.
- You can create a custom theme by extending the ThemeData class and passing it to the theme property of the MaterialApp widget.
- Themes can be accessed and customized throughout your app using the Theme.of(context) method.

Using Material Design:

- Flutter follows the Material Design guidelines, which provide a set of principles for designing intuitive and visually appealing apps.
- Flutter provides widgets that adhere to Material Design, such

as AppBar, Drawer, BottomNavigationBar, and more, making it easy to create apps that look and feel like native Android apps.

Creating Custom Widgets:

- Flutter allows you to create custom widgets to suit your app's specific needs.
- You can create custom widgets by extending the StatelessWidget or StatefulWidget class and implementing the build method to define the widget's UI.
- Custom widgets can encapsulate complex UI elements or behaviors, making your code more modular and maintainable.

Animation and Motion:

- Flutter provides powerful animation and motion APIs that allow you to create rich and interactive user experiences.
- You can use the AnimationController class to control animations and the Tween class to define the range of values to animate between.
- Flutter's AnimatedBuilder widget is useful for building complex animations that depend on the state of your app.

By leveraging Flutter's styling, theming, and animation capabilities, you can create beautiful and engaging user interfaces for your Flutter apps. These features empower developers to create apps that not only look great but also provide a smooth and delightful user experience.

Flutter UI Design With Examples:
Styling Your App:

- Styling individual widgets:

```dart
dart code
Text(
'Hello, World!',
style: TextStyle(
color: Colors.blue,
fontSize: 24.0,
fontWeight: FontWeight.bold,
),
)
```

- Using themes:

```dart
dart code
MaterialApp(
theme: ThemeData(
primaryColor: Colors.blue,
accentColor: Colors.green,
fontFamily: 'Roboto',
),
// Other app configurations
)
```

Working with Themes:

- Creating a custom theme:

```dart
dart code
ThemeData customTheme = ThemeData(
primaryColor: Colors.red,
accentColor: Colors.yellow,
fontFamily: 'Montserrat',
);
```

- Accessing and using a theme:

```dart
dart code
Text(
'Hello, World!',
style: Theme.of(context).textTheme.headline1,
```

```
)
```

Using Material Design:

- Using Material Design widgets:

```dart
dart code
MaterialApp(
home: Scaffold(
appBar: AppBar(
title: Text('My App'),
),
body: Center(
child: Text('Hello, World!'),
),
),
)
```

Creating Custom Widgets:

- Creating a custom button widget:

```dart
dart code
class CustomButton extends StatelessWidget {
@override
Widget build(BuildContext context) {
return FlatButton(
onPressed: () {
// Button logic
},
child: Text('Custom Button'),
);
}
}
```

- Using the custom button widget:

```dart
dart code
CustomButton(),
```

Animation and Motion:

- Creating a simple animation:

```dart
dart code
class MyAnimatedWidget extends StatefulWidget {
@override
_MyAnimatedWidgetState createState() => _MyAnimatedWidgetState();
}
class _MyAnimatedWidgetState extends State<MyAnimatedWidget> with SingleTickerProviderStateMixin {
late AnimationController _controller;
late Animation<double> _animation;
@override
void initState() {
super.initState();
_controller = AnimationController(duration: Duration(seconds: 1), vsync: this);
_animation = Tween<double>(begin: 0, end: 1).animate(_controller);
_controller.forward();
}
@override
Widget build(BuildContext context) {
return FadeTransition(
opacity: _animation,
child: Text('Animated Text'),
);
}
@override
void dispose() {
_controller.dispose();
super.dispose();
}
}
}
```

- Using the animated widget:

```dart
dart code
```

MyAnimatedWidget(),

These examples demonstrate how to apply styling, themes, Material Design, custom widgets, and animations in Flutter to create visually appealing and interactive user interfaces.

Styling your app in Flutter involves applying visual properties like colors, fonts, and sizes to your widgets to achieve a desired look and feel. Flutter provides a flexible styling system that allows you to customize the appearance of your app at both the widget and application levels. Let's dive deep into styling in Flutter:

1. Widget-level styling:

- You can style individual widgets using their respective style properties. For example, the Text widget has a style property that takes a TextStyle object.

```dart
dart code
Text(
'Hello, World!',
style: TextStyle(
color: Colors.blue,
fontSize: 24.0,
fontWeight: FontWeight.bold,
),
)
```

- In this example, we're setting the text color to blue, font size to 24.0, and font weight to bold.

2. Using themes:

- Flutter's Theme widget allows you to define a set of styles that can be applied globally to your app. This makes it easy to maintain a consistent look and feel across your app.
- You can define a theme in your MaterialApp widget and access it using the Theme.of(context) method.

```
dart code
MaterialApp(
theme: ThemeData(
primaryColor: Colors.blue,
accentColor: Colors.green,
fontFamily: 'Roboto',
),
// Other app configurations
)
```

- In this example, we're setting the primary color to blue, accent color to green, and the default font family to Roboto for our entire app.

3. Customizing themes:

- You can customize the theme further by creating a custom ThemeData object with your desired styles.

```
dart code
ThemeData customTheme = ThemeData(
primaryColor: Colors.red,
accentColor: Colors.yellow,
fontFamily: 'Montserrat',
);
```

- This custom theme can then be applied to your app using the theme property of the MaterialApp widget.

4. Accessing theme properties:

- Once you've defined a theme, you can access its properties throughout your app using the Theme.of(context) method.

```
dart code
Text(
```

```
'Hello, World!',
style: Theme.of(context).textTheme.headline1,
)
```

- In this example, we're accessing the headline1 text style defined in our theme and applying it to a Text widget.

5. Conclusion:

- Styling your app in Flutter involves applying visual properties to your widgets using the style property or using themes to define a consistent look and feel for your app.
- Flutter's styling system is flexible and allows for easy customization, making it easy to create visually appealing and consistent user interfaces across your app.

Working with Themes

Working with themes in Flutter allows you to define a set of consistent visual properties for your app, such as colors, fonts, and shapes. Themes help maintain a cohesive look and feel across your app and make it easy to update the styling in one place. Here's how you can work with themes in Flutter:

1. Defining a Theme:

- You can define a theme for your app by creating a ThemeData object. This object contains properties for various aspects of your app's styling, such as colors, typography, and shapes.

```dart
dart code
ThemeData(
primaryColor: Colors.blue,
accentColor: Colors.green,
fontFamily: 'Roboto',
)
```

- In this example, we're setting the primary color to blue, the accent color to green, and the default font family to Roboto.

2. Applying a Theme:

- To apply a theme to your app, you can use the theme property of the MaterialApp widget.

```dart
dart code
MaterialApp(
theme: ThemeData(
primaryColor: Colors.blue,
```

```dart
accentColor: Colors.green,
fontFamily: 'Roboto',
),
// Other app configurations
)
```

- This sets the theme for the entire app. Any widgets that use the Theme.of(context) method will inherit the styles defined in this theme.

3. Accessing Theme Properties:

- You can access the properties of the current theme using the Theme.of(context) method. This allows you to apply theme styles to individual widgets.

```dart
dart code
Text(
'Hello, World!',
style: Theme.of(context).textTheme.headline1,
)
```

- In this example, we're using the headline1 text style from the current theme to style a Text widget.

4. Customizing Themes:

- You can customize the theme further by creating a custom ThemeData object and passing it to the theme property of the MaterialApp widget.

```dart
dart code
ThemeData customTheme = ThemeData(
primaryColor: Colors.red,
accentColor: Colors.yellow,
fontFamily: 'Montserrat',
```

```
);
```

- This allows you to override specific properties of the default theme and apply your custom styles to the app.

5. Conclusion:

- Working with themes in Flutter allows you to define a consistent visual style for your app and easily apply it to your widgets. Themes help maintain a cohesive design across your app and make it easy to update the styling in one place.

Creating Custom Widgets

Creating custom widgets in Flutter allows you to build reusable components that encapsulate specific functionality or design patterns. Custom widgets can range from simple UI elements to complex interactive components. Here's how you can create custom widgets in Flutter:

1. Extending StatelessWidget or StatefulWidget:

- To create a custom widget, you typically extend either the StatelessWidget or StatefulWidget class, depending on whether your widget needs to manage state.
- Here's an example of a custom CustomButton widget that extends StatelessWidget:

```dart
dart code
class CustomButton extends StatelessWidget {
@override
Widget build(BuildContext context) {
return FlatButton(
onPressed: () {
// Button logic
},
child: Text('Custom Button'),
);
}
}
```

2. Implementing the build() method:

- In your custom widget class, you must implement the build() method, which returns the widget's UI representation.
- Inside the build() method, you can return any widget or

combination of widgets to define your custom widget's appearance and behavior.

3. Using the custom widget:

- Once you've defined your custom widget, you can use it in your app like any other widget.
- For example, you can add your CustomButton widget to the app's widget tree:

```dart
dart code
MaterialApp(
home: Scaffold(
body: Center(
child: CustomButton(),
),
),
)
```

4. Adding properties and parameters:

- Custom widgets can accept parameters to customize their behavior or appearance.
- You can define properties in your custom widget class and pass values to them when you use the widget.
- For example, you can modify the CustomButton widget to accept a custom text color:

```dart
dart code
class CustomButton extends StatelessWidget {
final Color textColor;
const CustomButton({Key? key, required this.textColor}) : super(key: key);
@override
Widget build(BuildContext context) {
return FlatButton(
onPressed: () {
// Button logic
```

```
},
child: Text(
'Custom Button',
style: TextStyle(color: textColor),
),
);
}
}
```

5. Reusing and composing widgets:

- Custom widgets can be reused across your app and composed together to create more complex UIs.
- By creating small, reusable widgets, you can build a modular and maintainable app architecture.

6. Conclusion:

- Creating custom widgets in Flutter allows you to build reusable components that encapsulate specific functionality or design patterns.
- By extending StatelessWidget or StatefulWidget and implementing the build() method, you can define the appearance and behavior of your custom widgets.
- Custom widgets can accept parameters to customize their appearance or behavior, making them versatile and easy to reuse across your app.

Animation and Motion

Animation and motion bring life and interactivity to your Flutter applications, making them more engaging and user-friendly. Flutter provides a rich set of tools and widgets to create animations, from simple transitions to complex, interactive animations. Here's an overview of animation and motion in Flutter:

1. Animation Basics:

- Animation in Flutter is achieved by changing the properties of widgets over time.
- The Animation class defines a range of values that can be animated, and the AnimationController class manages the animation's duration, curve, and status.

2. Tween Animation:

- The Tween class defines a range of values to animate between.
- For example, a Tween<double> can animate a double value from one value to another.
- You can define a Tween like this:

```dart
dart code
final Animation<double> animation = Tween<double>(
begin: 0.0,
end: 1.0,
).animate(controller);
```

3. Curved Animation:

- The CurvedAnimation class applies an easing curve to the animation, controlling the speed of the animation over time.

- You can define a CurvedAnimation like this:

```dart
dart code
final Animation<double> animation = CurvedAnimation(
parent: controller,
curve: Curves.easeInOut,
);
```

4. AnimatedBuilder Widget:

- The AnimatedBuilder widget is used to rebuild a part of the UI tree when the animation value changes.
- Wrap your animated widget with an AnimatedBuilder and pass the animation and builder function:

```dart
dart code
AnimatedBuilder(
animation: animation,
builder: (BuildContext context, Widget? child) {
return Opacity(
opacity: animation.value,
child: Text('Animated Text'),
);
},
)
```

5. AnimationController:

- The AnimationController class manages the animation's lifecycle, including starting, stopping, and resetting the animation.
- You can control the animation using methods like forward(), reverse(), and stop():

```dart
dart code
controller.forward(); // Start the animation
controller.reverse(); // Reverse the animation
controller.stop(); // Stop the animation
```

6. Disposing Animations:

- It's important to dispose of your animation controller when it's no longer needed to free up resources:

```dart
dart code
@override
void dispose() {
controller.dispose();
super.dispose();
}
```

7. Conclusion:

- Animation and motion in Flutter can greatly enhance the user experience by adding visual interest and interactivity to your applications.
- With Flutter's rich animation framework, you can create a wide range of animations, from simple fades to complex, interactive animations, bringing your app to life and providing a more engaging user experience.

Data Management in Flutter: Working with API

In Flutter, working with APIs (Application Programming Interfaces) is essential for fetching and sending data to remote servers. APIs allow your Flutter app to communicate with web servers, retrieve data, and update information. Here's how you can manage data in Flutter using APIs:

1. Using HTTP Package:

- Flutter provides the http package to make HTTP requests to APIs.
- You can use the http.get() or http.post() methods to fetch data from or send data to APIs, respectively.
- Example of fetching data from an API:

```dart
dart code
import 'package:http/http.dart' as http;
Future<void> fetchData() async {
var response = await http.get(Uri.parse('https://api.example.com/data'));
if (response.statusCode == 200) {
// Data fetched successfully
print(response.body);
} else {
// Failed to fetch data
print('Failed to fetch data: ${response.statusCode}');
}
}
```

2. Working with JSON Data:

- APIs often return data in JSON format, which you can easily parse in Flutter.

- Use the dart:convert package to encode and decode JSON data.
- Example of decoding JSON data fetched from an API:

```dart
dart code
import 'dart:convert';
Future<void> fetchData() async {
var response = await http.get(Uri.parse('https://api.example.com/data'));
if (response.statusCode == 200) {
var jsonData = jsonDecode(response.body);
print(jsonData);
} else {
print('Failed to fetch data: ${response.statusCode}');
}
}
```

3. Error Handling and Exception Handling:

- Handle errors and exceptions that may occur during API calls to ensure your app remains stable.
- Use try-catch blocks to catch and handle exceptions.
- Example of error handling in API calls:

```dart
dart code
try {
var response = await http.get(Uri.parse('https://api.example.com/data'));
if (response.statusCode == 200) {
// Data fetched successfully
print(response.body);
} else {
// Failed to fetch data
print('Failed to fetch data: ${response.statusCode}');
}
} catch (e) {
print('Error fetching data: $e');
}
```

4. Using Third-Party Libraries:

- Flutter provides several third-party libraries, such as dio and http for HTTP requests, that offer additional features and functionalities.
- Research and choose a library that best suits your project's requirements.

5. State Management:

- When working with APIs, you'll often need to manage the state of your app to reflect changes in data.
- Consider using state management solutions like Provider, Bloc, or Riverpod to manage and update your app's state based on API responses.

6. Conclusion:

- Working with APIs in Flutter is essential for fetching and sending data to remote servers.
- Use the http package to make HTTP requests and handle responses from APIs.
- Always handle errors and exceptions that may occur during API calls to ensure your app remains stable.
- Consider using third-party libraries for additional features and functionalities, and use state management solutions to manage your app's state based on API responses.

Parsing JSON Data

In Flutter, parsing JSON (JavaScript Object Notation) data is a common task when working with APIs. JSON is a lightweight data interchange format that is easy for humans to read and write and easy for machines to parse and generate. Here's how you can parse JSON data in Flutter:

1. Importing the Dart Convert Library:

- First, you need to import the dart:convert library, which provides support for JSON encoding and decoding.

```dart
dart code
import 'dart:convert';
```

2. Decoding JSON Data:

- Use the jsonDecode() function to decode a JSON string into a Dart object. This function returns a Map<String, dynamic> object.

```dart
dart code
String jsonString = '{"name": "John", "age": 30}';
Map<String, dynamic> data = jsonDecode(jsonString);
print(data['name']); // Output: John
print(data['age']); // Output: 30
```

3. Encoding Dart Objects to JSON:

- Use the jsonEncode() function to encode a Dart object into a JSON string.

```dart
dart code
Map<String, dynamic> data = {
```

```dart
'name': 'Jane',
'age': 25,
};
String jsonString = jsonEncode(data);
print(jsonString); // Output: {"name":"Jane","age":25}
```

4. Handling JSON Arrays:

- JSON arrays are represented as List<dynamic> objects in Dart.

```dart
dart code
String jsonArray = '[{"name": "Alice"}, {"name": "Bob"}]';
List<dynamic> dataList = jsonDecode(jsonArray);
print(dataList[0]['name']); // Output: Alice
print(dataList[1]['name']); // Output: Bob
```

5. Handling Nested JSON:

- Nested JSON objects can be accessed using multiple indexers or keys.

```dart
dart code
String nestedJson = '{"person": {"name": "Alice", "age": 30}}';
Map<String, dynamic> nestedData = jsonDecode(nestedJson);
print(nestedData['person']['name']); // Output: Alice
print(nestedData['person']['age']); // Output: 30
```

6. Error Handling:

- When parsing JSON data, it's important to handle errors that may occur, such as invalid JSON syntax.

```dart
dart code
try {
var data = jsonDecode('invalid json');
} catch (e) {
print('Error parsing JSON: $e');
}
```

7. Conclusion:

- Parsing JSON data in Flutter is straightforward using the dart:convert library.
- Use jsonDecode() to decode JSON strings into Dart objects and jsonEncode() to encode Dart objects into JSON strings.
- Handle errors that may occur during JSON parsing to ensure your app remains stable.

State Management Techniques (Provider, Bloc)

Using SQLite for Local Data Storage
SQLite is a lightweight, file-based relational database system that is widely used for local data storage in Flutter apps. It provides a simple and efficient way to store and retrieve structured data locally on the user's device. Here's how you can use SQLite for local data storage in Flutter:

1. Add Dependencies:

- First, add the sqflite and path_provider dependencies to your pubspec.yaml file.

```yaml
yaml code
dependencies:
flutter:
sdk: flutter
sqflite: ^2.0.0
path_provider: ^2.0.2
```

2. Initialize the Database:

- Create a class to manage your SQLite database. Open the database and create tables if they don't exist.

```dart
dart code
import 'package:sqflite/sqflite.dart';
import 'package:path_provider/path_provider.dart';
import 'package:path/path.dart';
class DatabaseHelper {
static Database? _database;
static const String tableName = 'contacts';
```

```dart
Future<Database> get database async {
if (_database != null) {
return _database!;
}
_database = await initDatabase();
return _database!;
}
Future<Database> initDatabase() async {
var documentsDirectory = await getApplicationDocumentsDirectory();
var path = join(documentsDirectory.path, 'my_database.db');
return await openDatabase(
path,
version: 1,
onCreate: (db, version) {
return db.execute(
'CREATE TABLE $tableName(id INTEGER PRIMARY KEY, name TEXT,
phone TEXT)',
);
},
);
}
}
```

3. Insert Data:

- Use the insert() method to insert data into the database.

dart code
```dart
Future<void> insertContact(Contact contact) async {
final db = await database;
await db.insert(tableName, contact.toMap());
}
```

4. Retrieve Data:

- Use the query() method to retrieve data from the database.

dart code
```dart
Future<List<Contact>> getContacts() async {
final db = await database;
```

```dart
final List<Map<String, dynamic>> maps = await db.query(tableName);
return List.generate(maps.length, (i) {
return Contact(
id: maps[i]['id'],
name: maps[i]['name'],
phone: maps[i]['phone'],
);
});
}
```

5. Update Data:

- Use the update() method to update existing data in the database.

```dart
dart code
Future<void> updateContact(Contact contact) async {
final db = await database;
await db.update(
tableName,
contact.toMap(),
where: 'id = ?',
whereArgs: [contact.id],
);
}
```

6. Delete Data:

- Use the delete() method to delete data from the database.

```dart
dart code
Future<void> deleteContact(int id) async {
final db = await database;
await db.delete(
tableName,
where: 'id = ?',
whereArgs: [id],
);
}
```

7. Conclusion:

- SQLite provides a convenient way to store and retrieve structured data locally in Flutter apps.
- Use the sqflite package to interact with the SQLite database and perform operations such as inserting, retrieving, updating, and deleting data.
- Ensure proper error handling and database management practices to maintain data integrity and app stability.

Introduction to Firebase

Firebase is a comprehensive platform developed by Google for building mobile and web applications. It provides a variety of tools and services that help developers develop high-quality apps, grow their user base, and earn more revenue. Firebase offers features like real-time database, authentication, cloud storage, hosting, analytics, and more, all in one integrated platform. Here's an introduction to some of the key features of Firebase:

1. Realtime Database: Firebase Realtime Database is a cloud-hosted NoSQL database that allows developers to store and sync data between users in real-time. It's ideal for applications that require real-time updates, such as chat apps, collaborative apps, and multiplayer games.

2. Authentication: Firebase Authentication provides easy-to-use authentication services to verify users and manage their authentication state. It supports various authentication methods like email/password, phone number, Google, Facebook, Twitter, and more.

3. Cloud Firestore: Cloud Firestore is a flexible, scalable database for mobile, web, and server development from Firebase and Google Cloud Platform. It keeps data in sync across client apps through realtime listeners and offers offline support for mobile and web apps.

4. Cloud Storage: Firebase Cloud Storage provides a secure and reliable way to store and serve user-generated content, such as photos and videos, in your apps. It integrates seamlessly with Firebase Authentication to manage access permissions.

5. Hosting: Firebase Hosting provides fast and secure hosting for web apps and static content. It offers features like custom domain support, SSL encryption, and continuous deployment with GitHub, Bitbucket, or GitLab.

6. Analytics: Firebase Analytics helps you understand user behavior and app performance. It provides insights into user engagement, retention, and conversion, allowing you to make data-driven decisions to improve your app.

7. Cloud Functions: Firebase Cloud Functions allow you to run backend code in response to events triggered by Firebase features and HTTPS requests. It lets you extend the functionality of your app without managing servers.

8. Remote Config: Firebase Remote Config allows you to change the behavior and appearance of your app without publishing an app update. You can tailor the user experience based on factors like user segmentation, language, or region.

9. Performance Monitoring: Firebase Performance Monitoring provides insights into your app's performance, including metrics like app startup time, network performance, and UI rendering. It helps you identify and fix performance issues to provide a better user experience.

10. A/B Testing: Firebase A/B Testing allows you to test different app configurations and features with your users to determine which ones perform better. It helps you make informed decisions to improve your app's performance and user engagement.

Firebase provides a powerful and integrated set of tools and services that help developers build high-quality apps quickly and efficiently. It's suitable for a wide range of applications, from small personal projects to large-scale enterprise applications.

Firebase Authentication

Firebase Authentication is a service provided by Firebase that allows you to easily add user authentication to your app. It offers multiple authentication methods, such as email/password, phone number, Google, Facebook, Twitter, and more, making it flexible and convenient for users to sign in. Here's an overview of Firebase Authentication:

1. Sign-In Methods:

- Firebase Authentication supports various sign-in methods, including email/password, phone number, Google, Facebook, Twitter, GitHub, Apple, and more.
- You can enable multiple sign-in methods in your app to offer users a choice of how they want to sign in.

2. User Management:

- Firebase Authentication provides APIs to manage user accounts, such as creating new users, updating user profiles, and deleting users.
- You can also manage user sessions and revoke tokens to force users to sign in again.

3. Secure Authentication:

- Firebase Authentication uses industry-standard security practices to ensure user data is protected.
- It encrypts passwords and sensitive data and securely stores user credentials.

4. Custom Authentication:

- Firebase Authentication allows you to integrate custom authentication systems with your app.
- You can use Firebase Authentication with existing authentication systems or create your own authentication mechanism.

5. OAuth Providers:

- Firebase Authentication supports OAuth providers like Google, Facebook, Twitter, and GitHub.
- This allows users to sign in with their existing accounts on these platforms.

6. Anonymous Authentication:

- Firebase Authentication supports anonymous sign-in, allowing users to use your app without requiring them to create an account.
- You can later convert anonymous accounts to permanent accounts when the user decides to sign up.

7. Email Verification and Password Recovery:

- Firebase Authentication provides APIs for email verification and password recovery.
- Users can verify their email address to gain access to certain features and recover their password if they forget it.

8. Integration with Other Firebase Services:

- Firebase Authentication seamlessly integrates with other

Firebase services, such as Firestore, Realtime Database, and Cloud Functions.
- This allows you to use authentication information to personalize user experiences and secure access to resources.

9. Firebase Console:

- Firebase Authentication provides a console where you can manage users, view authentication logs, and configure authentication settings for your app.

10. Conclusion:

- Firebase Authentication simplifies the process of adding user authentication to your app, offering a range of sign-in methods and secure authentication practices.
- It helps you build a secure and user-friendly authentication system for your app, enhancing the user experience and security of your app.

Firestore Database Overview:

Firestore is a flexible, scalable database for mobile, web, and server development from Firebase and Google Cloud Platform. It's a NoSQL document database that lets you store, sync, and query data for your applications. Firestore is designed to work offline and online, making it ideal for real-time applications.

Key Concepts:

1. **Documents:** Data in Firestore is stored in documents, which are JSON-like objects. Each document contains a set of key-value pairs, where each key is a field name and each value is the field's value. Documents are stored in collections.
2. **Collections:** Collections are containers for documents. You can think of them as folders that contain related documents. Collections can also contain subcollections, allowing for hierarchical data structures.
3. **Fields:** Fields are the key-value pairs within a document. Each field has a name and a value. Fields can contain simple data types like strings, numbers, and booleans, as well as more complex data types like arrays and nested objects.
4. **Queries:** Firestore supports powerful queries for retrieving data. You can query documents based on their fields, sort and filter the results, and limit the number of documents returned.
5. **Realtime Updates:** One of the key features of Firestore is its support for realtime updates. When data in the database changes, clients that are listening to those changes are notified in real-time, allowing them to update their UIs

accordingly.

Using Firestore in Flutter:

To use Firestore in your Flutter app, you first need to add the cloud_firestore dependency to your pubspec.yaml file:

```yaml
yaml code
dependencies:
flutter:
sdk: flutter
cloud_firestore: ^2.5.0
```

Then, you can use the FirebaseFirestore class to interact with Firestore. Here's an example of how to add data to Firestore:

```dart
dart code
import 'package:cloud_firestore/cloud_firestore.dart';
void addData() {
FirebaseFirestore.instance
.collection('users')
.doc('ABC123')
.set({'name': 'John Doe', 'age': 30})
.then((_) => print('Added'))
.catchError((error) => print('Error: $error'));
}
```

In this example, we're adding a document with the ID ABC123 to the users collection with the fields name and age. The set() method is used to add data to Firestore.

Illustration:

Imagine you have a Firestore database for a simple blogging app. You might have a posts collection, where each document represents a blog post. Each post document could have fields like title, author, content, and timestamp.

When a new blog post is created in your app, you would add a new document to the posts collection with the post's details. Clients that are listening to the posts collection would receive realtime updates whenever a new post is added, allowing them to display the new post in their UIs immediately.

Firebase Cloud Messaging

Firebase Cloud Messaging (FCM) is a cross-platform messaging solution that allows you to send notifications and messages to users across various platforms, including Android, iOS, and web. It provides a reliable and scalable way to deliver messages to your app users, whether they are using your app or not. Here's an overview of Firebase Cloud Messaging with explanations, examples, and illustrations:

1. Overview of Firebase Cloud Messaging:

Firebase Cloud Messaging (FCM) allows you to send notifications and messages to users across different platforms, including Android, iOS, and web. It supports two types of messages:

- **Notification Messages:** These are handled by the system tray and are used to alert users of new messages or events, even when the app is in the background.
- **Data Messages:** These are handled by the app's code and can be used to trigger custom actions or update app data.

2. Key Concepts:

- **Message:** A message is a data structure that contains the content to be sent to the user's device. It can include a title, body, and other custom data.
- **Token:** A token is a unique identifier for a specific instance of your app on a device. It is used to route messages to the correct device.
- **Topic:** A topic is a way to group devices that are interested in a particular subject. You can subscribe devices to topics, and

then send messages to the topic, which will be delivered to all subscribed devices.

3. Sending Messages:

To send a message using FCM, you need to use the Firebase Admin SDK or the Firebase Console. Here's an example of sending a notification message using the Firebase Admin SDK in Node.js:

```javascript
javascript code
const admin = require('firebase-admin');
const serviceAccount = require('path/to/serviceAccountKey.json');
admin.initializeApp({
credential: admin.credential.cert(serviceAccount)
});
const message = {
notification: {
title: 'New Message',
body: 'You have a new message!'
},
token: 'device_token_here'
};
admin.messaging().send(message)
.then((response) => {
console.log('Successfully sent message:', response);
})
.catch((error) => {
console.log('Error sending message:', error);
});
```

4. Receiving Messages:

To receive messages in your app, you need to implement a message handler. On Android, you can use a FirebaseMessagingService to handle incoming messages. On iOS, you can use the didReceiveRemoteNotification method to handle notifications.

5. Illustration:

Imagine you have a news app that uses Firebase Cloud Messaging to send breaking news notifications to users. When a new article is published, you send a notification message to all subscribed devices.

The message contains the title and body of the article. Users receive the notification on their devices and can tap on it to open the app and read the article.

6. Conclusion:

Firebase Cloud Messaging is a powerful tool for sending notifications and messages to users across different platforms. It provides a reliable and scalable way to engage with your app users and keep them informed about important events. By integrating FCM into your app, you can enhance the user experience and drive user engagement.

Accessing Device Sensors (Camera, GPS)

In Flutter, you can access device sensors like the camera and GPS using various plugins. These plugins provide APIs to interact with the device's hardware and retrieve sensor data. Here's how you can access the camera and GPS sensors in Flutter:

1. Camera:

- Use the camera plugin to access the device's camera and take photos or record videos.
- Add the camera dependency to your pubspec.yaml file:

```yaml
yaml code
dependencies:
flutter:
sdk: flutter
camera: ^0.9.4+5
```

- Use the CameraController class to control the camera and capture photos or videos:

```dart
dart code
import 'package:camera/camera.dart';
Future<void> initCamera() async {
final cameras = await availableCameras();
final camera = cameras.first;
final controller = CameraController(camera, ResolutionPreset.medium);
await controller.initialize();
// Use the controller to take photos or record videos
}
```

2. GPS (Location):

- Use the location plugin to access the device's GPS sensor and retrieve the device's location.
- Add the location dependency to your pubspec.yaml file:

```yaml
yaml code
dependencies:
flutter:
sdk: flutter
location: ^4.3.0
```

- Use the Location class to retrieve the device's location:

```dart
dart code
import 'package:location/location.dart';
Future<void> getLocation() async {
final location = Location();
final currentLocation = await location.getLocation();
print('Latitude: ${currentLocation.latitude}, Longitude: ${currentLocation.longitude}');
}
```

3. Permissions:

- Remember to request the necessary permissions from the user to access the camera and GPS sensors. Use the permission_handler package to request permissions:

```dart
dart code
import 'package:permission_handler/permission_handler.dart';
Future<void> requestPermissions() async {
final cameraStatus = await Permission.camera.request();
final locationStatus = await Permission.location.request();
if (cameraStatus.isGranted && locationStatus.isGranted) {
// Permissions granted, you can now access the camera and GPS sensors
}
}
```

4. Conclusion:

- By using plugins like camera and location, you can easily access the device's camera and GPS sensors in Flutter.
- Remember to handle permissions properly and check for permission status before accessing the sensors.

Using Device Permissions

In Flutter, you can request and check for device permissions using the permission_handler package. This package provides a simple API to request permissions and check their status. Here's how you can use it to manage permissions in your Flutter app:

1. Add the Dependency:

- First, add the permission_handler dependency to your pubspec.yaml file:

```yaml
yaml code
dependencies:
flutter:
sdk: flutter
permission_handler: ^8.2.8
```

2. Requesting Permissions:

- Use the request method to request permissions from the user. You can request multiple permissions at once:

```dart
dart code
import 'package:permission_handler/permission_handler.dart';
Future<void> requestPermissions() async {
var status = await Permission.camera.request();
if (status.isGranted) {
// Permission granted, you can now access the camera
} else {
// Permission denied, handle accordingly
}
}
```

3. Checking Permission Status:

- Use the status method to check the status of a permission:

```dart
dart code
Future<bool> checkCameraPermission() async {
var status = await Permission.camera.status;
return status.isGranted;
}
```

4. Handling Permission Results:

- You can handle the permission request result in the same method where you requested the permission:

```dart
dart code
Future<void> requestPermissions() async {
var status = await Permission.camera.request();
if (status.isGranted) {
// Permission granted, you can now access the camera
} else {
// Permission denied, show a message or request again
}
}
```

5. Conclusion:

- The permission_handler package provides a simple way to manage permissions in your Flutter app.
- Always request permissions when they are needed and handle permission denied scenarios gracefully to provide a better user experience.

Integrating with Platform-Specific Code (Platform Channels)

In Flutter, you can integrate platform-specific code using platform channels. Platform channels allow you to communicate between your Flutter app and platform-specific code written in Java (for Android) or Objective-C/Swift (for iOS). This enables you to access native features and APIs that are not available in Flutter. Here's how you can integrate platform-specific code using platform channels:

1. Define a Method Channel:

- Define a method channel in your Dart code to communicate with the platform-specific code. This channel will have a unique name that identifies it.

```dart
dart code
import 'package:flutter/services.dart';
final MethodChannel _channel = MethodChannel('com.example.myapp/mychannel');
```

2. Invoke Platform-Specific Code:

- Use the invokeMethod method on the method channel to invoke platform-specific code. You can pass arguments to the platform code and receive a result back.

```dart
dart code
Future<void> platformSpecificMethod() async {
try {
final String result = await _channel.invokeMethod('myPlatformMethod');
print('Platform-specific result: $result');
} on PlatformException catch (e) {
```

```
print('Error invoking platform-specific method: ${e.message}');
}
}
```

3. Implement Platform-Specific Code:

- Implement the platform-specific code in Java (for Android) or Objective-C/Swift (for iOS). This code should handle the method invocation and return a result if needed.
    - Android (Java):

```java
java code
public class MyPlugin implements MethodCallHandler {
@Override
public void onMethodCall(MethodCall call, Result result) {
if (call.method.equals("myPlatformMethod")) {
// Handle method call and return a result if needed
result.success("Hello from Android");
} else {
result.notImplemented();
}
}
}
```

- iOS (Swift):

```swift
swift code
class MyPlugin: NSObject, FlutterPlugin {
static func register(with registrar: FlutterPluginRegistrar) {
let channel = FlutterMethodChannel(name: "com.example.myapp/mychannel",
binaryMessenger: registrar.messenger())
let instance = MyPlugin()
registrar.addMethodCallDelegate(instance, channel: channel)
}
func handle(_ call: FlutterMethodCall, result: @escaping FlutterResult) {
if call.method == "myPlatformMethod" {
// Handle method call and return a result if needed
result("Hello from iOS")
```

```
} else {
result(FlutterMethodNotImplemented)
}
}
}
```

4. Register the Plugin:

- Register the plugin in your Flutter app's main method to
  make it available for use.
    - Android (Java):

```
java code
MyPlugin.registerWith(registrarFor("com.example.myapp/mychannel"));
```

- iOS (Swift):

```
swift code
MyPlugin.register(with: self)
```

5. Use the Platform-Specific Code:

- Finally, you can use the platform-specific code in your Flutter
  app by calling the platformSpecificMethod method.

```
dart code
platformSpecificMethod();
```

6. Conclusion:

- Platform channels allow you to integrate platform-specific
  code into your Flutter app, enabling you to access native
  features and APIs that are not available in Flutter.
- Use platform channels carefully and consider using them only
  when necessary, as they can introduce platform-specific
  dependencies and increase complexity.

Unit Testing

Unit testing is a crucial part of the development process that involves testing individual units or components of your code to ensure they work correctly in isolation. In Flutter, you can use the built-in flutter_test package to write and run unit tests for your Dart code. Here's how you can write unit tests in Flutter:

1. Adding the flutter_test **Dependency:**

- First, ensure that the flutter_test package is included in your dev_dependencies in the pubspec.yaml file:

```yaml
yaml code
dev_dependencies:
flutter_test:
sdk: flutter
```

2. Writing a Unit Test:

- Create a new Dart file for your unit tests (e.g., my_widget_test.dart) and import the necessary packages:

```dart
dart code
import 'package:flutter_test/flutter_test.dart';
void main() {
test('MyWidget should do something', () {
// Your test logic here
});
}
```

3. Writing Test Logic:

- Write the test logic inside the test function. This logic typically involves creating instances of your classes and calling methods to verify their behavior:

```dart
dart code
import 'package:flutter_test/flutter_test.dart';
class MyWidget {
int add(int a, int b) => a + b;
}
void main() {
test('MyWidget should add two numbers', () {
final widget = MyWidget();
expect(widget.add(1, 2), 3);
});
}
```

4. Running Tests:

- You can run your unit tests using the flutter test command in the terminal. Make sure your device or emulator is connected:

```bash
bash code
flutter test
```

5. Assertions and Matchers:

- Use the expect function to assert that certain conditions are true. You can also use matchers for more complex assertions:

```dart
dart code
test('MyWidget should have a positive value', () {
final widget = MyWidget();
expect(widget.add(1, 2), isPositive);
});
```

6. Mocking Dependencies:

- Use packages like mockito to mock dependencies and control their behavior during testing. This allows you to isolate the unit under test and focus on its behavior:

```dart
dart code
import 'package:mockito/mockito.dart';
class MockDependency extends Mock implements MyDependency {}
void main() {
test('MyWidget should use dependency', () {
final dependency = MockDependency();
when(dependency.getValue()).thenReturn(42);
final widget = MyWidget(dependency);
expect(widget.value, 42);
});
}
```

7. Conclusion:

- Unit testing is essential for ensuring the correctness and reliability of your code. By writing unit tests in Flutter, you can catch bugs early, improve code quality, and make your app more robust and maintainable.

Widget Testing

I ntegration Testing
Integration testing in Flutter involves testing the interaction between different parts of your app, such as widgets, services, and external dependencies. It helps ensure that these components work together correctly and that your app behaves as expected. Here's how you can perform integration testing in Flutter:

1. Setting Up Integration Tests:

- Create a new directory for your integration tests (e.g., test_driver) in your Flutter project.
- Add the flutter_driver and test packages to your dev_dependencies in the pubspec.yaml file:

```yaml
yaml code
dev_dependencies:
flutter_driver:
sdk: flutter
test: any
```

- Create a new Dart file for your integration test (e.g., app_test.dart) in the test_driver directory.

2. Writing an Integration Test:

- Use the FlutterDriver class from the flutter_driver package to drive your app and interact with its widgets:

```dart
dart code
import 'package:flutter_driver/flutter_driver.dart';
```

```dart
import 'package:test/test.dart';
void main() {
group('MyApp', () {
FlutterDriver driver;
setUpAll(() async {
driver = await FlutterDriver.connect();
});
tearDownAll(() async {
if (driver != null) {
driver.close();
}
});
test('MyApp should display a welcome message', () async {
// Find the welcome message on the screen
final welcomeMessage = find.text('Welcome to MyApp');
// Verify that the welcome message is displayed
expect(await driver.getText(welcomeMessage), 'Welcome to MyApp');
});
});
}
```

3. Running Integration Tests:

- You can run your integration tests using the flutter drive command in the terminal. Make sure your device or emulator is connected:

```bash
bash code
flutter drive—target=test_driver/app.dart
```

4. Using Matchers and Assertions:

- Use the expect function and matchers to verify that your app behaves as expected. You can use matchers like find.text to locate widgets on the screen and expect to verify their properties:

```dart
dart code
expect(await driver.getText(find.text('Hello')), 'Hello');
```

5. Conclusion:

- Integration testing in Flutter allows you to test how different parts of your app work together. By writing integration tests, you can ensure that your app functions correctly and delivers a great user experience.

Debugging Techniques

Debugging is an essential skill for developers, helping them identify and fix issues in their code. In Flutter, you can use various techniques and tools to debug your app effectively. Here are some common debugging techniques:

1. Print Statements:

- Use print statements to output messages to the console. This can help you track the flow of your code and see the values of variables at different points in your app.

dart code
print('Debug message');

2. Debugging Tools:

- Use the debugging tools provided by Flutter, such as the Flutter DevTools and the built-in debugging features of IDEs like Android Studio and Visual Studio Code. These tools allow you to inspect the UI hierarchy, view logs, and debug your app's performance.
    - To open Flutter DevTools, run flutter pub global run devtools in your terminal and open the provided URL in your browser.
    - In Android Studio or Visual Studio Code, you can use the debugging features to set breakpoints, step through your code, and inspect variables.

3. Logging:

- Use logging libraries like logger to log messages at different log levels (e.g., debug, info, warning, error). This can help you organize your logs and filter them based on their importance.

dart code
logger.d('Debug message');

4. Exception Handling:

- Use try-catch blocks to catch and handle exceptions in your code. This can prevent your app from crashing and help you identify the source of the error.

dart code
```
try {
// Code that might throw an exception
} catch (e) {
// Handle the exception
print('Exception caught: $e');
}
```

5. Debugging Widgets:

- Use the flutter_debugger package to visually inspect your app's UI and debug layout issues. This package provides a set of tools that allow you to visualize the layout of your app and identify layout problems.
  - Add the flutter_debugger dependency to your pubspec.yaml file:

yaml code
```
dependencies:
flutter_debugger: ^1.0.0
```

- Import the package and use its widgets to debug your app's UI:

```dart
dart code
import 'package:flutter_debugger/flutter_debugger.dart';
// Wrap your app's root widget with the Debugger widget
void main() => runApp(Debugger(child: MyApp()));
```

6. Remote Debugging:

- Use remote debugging to debug your app running on a physical device. This allows you to connect your device to your development machine and debug your app as if it were running in an emulator or simulator.
    - Enable USB debugging on your device and connect it to your computer.
    - In Android Studio or Visual Studio Code, select your device from the list of devices and start a debugging session.

7. Conclusion:

- By using these debugging techniques and tools, you can effectively identify and fix issues in your Flutter app, ensuring a smoother development process and a better user experience.

Deploying Your Flutter App

Building for Android
To deploy your Flutter app to an Android device or emulator, you need to follow these steps:

1. **Configure Your Flutter Environment:**
   - Make sure you have Flutter installed and set up on your machine. You can follow the installation instructions on the Flutter website.

2. **Set Up Your Android Device or Emulator:**
   - If you're using a physical Android device, enable USB debugging in the developer options.
   - If you're using an Android emulator, make sure it's running and properly configured in Android Studio.

3. **Build Your Flutter App:**
   - Open a terminal and navigate to your Flutter project directory.
   - Run the following command to build your app for release:

code
```
flutter build apk
```

- This command will generate an APK file for your app in the build/app/outputs/flutter-apk directory.

1. **Deploy to Device:**
   - If you're using a physical Android device, connect it to your computer via USB.

- ◦ Run the following command to install the APK on your device:

Copy code
flutter install

- This command will install the APK on your connected device.

1. **Deploy to Emulator:**
   - ◦ If you're using an Android emulator, make sure it's running.
   - ◦ Run the following command to install the APK on your emulator:

Copy code
flutter install

- This command will install the APK on your running emulator.

1. **Run Your App:**
   - ◦ Once the installation is complete, you can run your app on the device or emulator by selecting it from the list of available devices in Android Studio or Visual Studio Code.
   - ◦ Alternatively, you can run the following command to start your app:

arduino code
flutter run

1. **Testing and Debugging:**
   - ◦ Once your app is running, you can test and debug it

on your Android device or emulator using the debugging tools provided by Flutter and your IDE.

2. **Conclusion:**
    - By following these steps, you can deploy your Flutter app to an Android device or emulator for testing and distribution.

Building for iOS

Publishing to Google Play Store

To publish your Flutter app to the Google Play Store, you need to follow these steps:

1. **Prepare Your App for Release:**
   - Update the version number and build number in your pubspec.yaml file.
   - Ensure that your app is ready for release, including testing on multiple devices and screen sizes.
2. **Generate an Android App Bundle (AAB):**
   - Open a terminal and navigate to your Flutter project directory.
   - Run the following command to generate an AAB file for your app:

Copy code
```
flutter build appbundle
```

- This command will generate an AAB file in the build/app/outputs/bundle/release directory.

1. **Create a Developer Account:**
   - If you don't already have one, create a developer account on the Google Play Console.
   - Pay the one-time registration fee (currently $25).
2. **Prepare Your Store Listing:**
   - Log in to the Google Play Console and create a new app.

- Enter the app's title, description, screenshots, and other details required for the store listing.
- Upload your app's icon and feature graphic.

3. **Upload Your AAB File:**
   - Go to the "App releases" section in the Google Play Console.
   - Click on "Manage" under the "Production" track.
   - Click on "Create Release" and upload your AAB file.

4. **Set Up Store Listing and Pricing:**
   - Fill out the "Store listing" section with information about your app, including a description, screenshots, and a promotional video (if available).
   - Set up pricing and distribution options for your app.

5. **Review and Rollout:**
   - Review the details of your app release and click "Review" to submit it for review.
   - Once your app is approved, you can rollout the release to users.

6. **Monitor and Update:**
   - Monitor your app's performance on the Google Play Console.
   - Update your app regularly to fix bugs and add new features.

7. **Conclusion:**
   - By following these steps, you can publish your Flutter app to the Google Play Store and make it available to millions of users worldwide.

Publishing to Apple App Store

To publish your Flutter app to the Apple App Store, you need to follow these steps:

1. **Prepare Your App for Release:**
   - Update the version number and build number in your pubspec.yaml file.
   - Ensure that your app is ready for release, including testing on multiple devices and screen sizes.
2. **Generate an iOS Archive:**
   - Open a terminal and navigate to your Flutter project directory.
   - Run the following command to generate an iOS archive:

```arduino
arduino code
flutter build ios—release
```

- This command will generate an iOS archive file in the build/ios/archive directory.

1. **Create an App Store Connect Record:**
   - Go to the App Store Connect website and log in with your Apple developer account.
   - Click on "My Apps" and then click on the "+" button to create a new app.
   - Fill in the details for your app, including the app name, bundle ID, and other required information.
2. **Prepare Your App for Submission:**

- Create an app store listing for your app, including a description, keywords, screenshots, and a promotional video (if available).
- Set up pricing and availability options for your app.

3. **Upload Your iOS Archive:**
   - In Xcode, open the Organizer window (Window > Organizer).
   - Select your iOS archive and click on the "Distribute App" button.
   - Follow the prompts to upload your archive to App Store Connect.

4. **Submit Your App for Review:**
   - In App Store Connect, go to the "App Store" tab and click on "iOS App."
   - Click on the "Prepare for Submission" button and fill in the required information, including app information, pricing, and availability.
   - Click on the "Submit for Review" button to submit your app for review by Apple.

5. **Monitor Your App's Review Status:**
   - Once you've submitted your app for review, you can monitor its status in the App Store Connect dashboard.
   - Apple will review your app to ensure it complies with the App Store guidelines. This process can take several days to a week or more.

6. **Release Your App:**
   - Once your app has been approved, you can release it to the App Store.
   - Go to the "App Store" tab in App Store Connect, select your app, and click on the "Release This Version" button.

7. **Conclusion:**
    ○ By following these steps, you can publish your Flutter app to the Apple App Store and make it available to iOS users worldwide.

Code Organization and Structure

Code organization and structure are crucial aspects of writing maintainable and scalable Flutter apps. Here's how you can organize and structure your Flutter code effectively:

1. Folder Structure:

- Flutter apps typically follow a common folder structure to organize different parts of the app. Here's a basic example:

css code

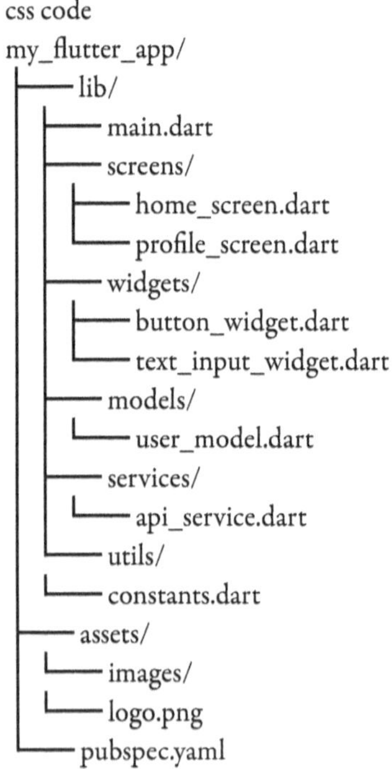

```
my_flutter_app/
├── lib/
│   ├── main.dart
│   ├── screens/
│   │   ├── home_screen.dart
│   │   └── profile_screen.dart
│   ├── widgets/
│   │   ├── button_widget.dart
│   │   └── text_input_widget.dart
│   ├── models/
│   │   └── user_model.dart
│   ├── services/
│   │   └── api_service.dart
│   ├── utils/
│   └── constants.dart
├── assets/
│   └── images/
│   └── logo.png
└── pubspec.yaml
```

2. Main.dart File:

- The main.dart file is the entry point of your Flutter app. It typically contains the main function and initializes the app's MaterialApp widget.

```dart
dart code
void main() {
runApp(MyApp());
}
class MyApp extends StatelessWidget {
@override
Widget build(BuildContext context) {
return MaterialApp(
title: 'My Flutter App',
home: HomeScreen(),
);
}
}
```

3. Screens:

- Screens represent different screens or pages of your app. Each screen should be a separate widget.

```dart
dart code
class HomeScreen extends StatelessWidget {
@override
Widget build(BuildContext context) {
return Scaffold(
appBar: AppBar(title: Text('Home')),
body: Center(
child: Text('Welcome to the Home Screen!'),
),
);
}
}
```

4. Widgets:

- Widgets are reusable UI components that can be used across different screens. It's a good practice to organize widgets into a separate folder.

```dart
dart code
class ButtonWidget extends StatelessWidget {
@override
Widget build(BuildContext context) {
return ElevatedButton(
onPressed: () {},
child: Text('Click Me'),
);
}
}
```

5. Models:

- Models represent the data structures used in your app. They help in organizing and managing app data effectively.

```dart
dart code
class User {
final String name;
final int age;
User({required this.name, required this.age});
}
```

6. Services:

- Services handle business logic and interactions with external services, such as APIs or databases.

```dart
dart code
class ApiService {
Future<User> fetchUser() async {
// API call to fetch user data
}
}
```

7. Utils:

- Utils contain utility functions, constants, or enums used

throughout your app.

```dart
dart code
class Constants {
static const double padding = 16.0;
static const String apiUrl = 'https://api.example.com';
}
```

8. Asset Management:

- Use the assets folder to store assets like images, fonts, and other resources used in your app.

```yaml
yaml code
flutter:
assets:
- assets/images/logo.png
```

9. Conclusion:

- Organizing your Flutter code in a structured manner makes it easier to maintain, debug, and scale your app as it grows. By following these guidelines, you can ensure that your Flutter app remains organized and maintainable throughout its development lifecycle.

Performance Optimization

Performance optimization is crucial for ensuring that your Flutter app runs smoothly and efficiently. Here are some key strategies for optimizing the performance of your Flutter app:

1. Reduce Widget Rebuilds:

- Use const constructors for stateless widgets and const variables wherever possible to prevent unnecessary widget rebuilds.
- Use const widgets for static UI components that don't change.

2. Minimize Widget Size:

- Break down complex widgets into smaller, more manageable widgets.
- Use ListView.builder or GridView.builder for large lists to only build widgets that are currently visible.

3. Avoid Excessive Nesting:

- Avoid nesting too many widgets inside each other, as it can lead to increased build times and decreased performance.
- Use layout widgets like Column, Row, Stack, and Flex judiciously to achieve the desired layout without unnecessary nesting.

4. Use Keys Wisely:

- Use keys to uniquely identify widgets when necessary, but avoid using them excessively as they can lead to performance issues.
- Use GlobalKey sparingly and only when absolutely necessary.

5. Optimize Image Loading:

- Use the cached_network_image package to cache images loaded from the network and reduce load times.
- Use smaller image sizes and compress images where possible to reduce the app's overall size.

6. Minimize Stateful Widgets:

- Use stateless widgets whenever possible to avoid the overhead of managing state.
- Use the provider package for managing state across your app efficiently.

7. Use const Widgets:

- Use const widgets wherever possible to create static widgets that don't need to be rebuilt.
- For example:

dart code
```
const MyWidget();
```

8. Avoid Expensive Operations in Build Methods:

- Avoid performing expensive operations, such as network requests or complex calculations, inside build methods.
- Perform these operations asynchronously and update the UI when the data is available.

9. Use Performance Profiling Tools:

- Use Flutter's built-in performance tools, such as the DevTools Performance tab or the flutter analyze command, to identify performance bottlenecks in your app.
- Use the flutter run—profile command to run your app in profile mode and analyze its performance.

10. Conclusion:

- By following these performance optimization techniques, you can ensure that your Flutter app runs smoothly and efficiently, providing a great user experience for your users.

Accessibility Guidelines

Accessibility is an important aspect of app development that ensures everyone, including users with disabilities, can access and use your app. Here are some guidelines for making your Flutter app more accessible:

1. Use Semantic Widgets:

- Use semantic widgets like Semantics, ExcludeSemantics, and MergeSemantics to provide meaningful information to screen readers.

2. Provide Descriptive Semantics:

- Use the label and hint properties of widgets to provide descriptive labels and hints for screen readers.

3. Ensure Focusability:

- Make sure all interactive elements, such as buttons and text fields, are focusable using the Focus widget or the focusable property.

4. Manage Focus Order:

- Use the FocusTraversalGroup widget to manage the focus order of interactive elements in your app.

5. Provide Keyboard Support:

- Ensure that all interactive elements can be accessed and

activated using the keyboard alone.

6. Use High Contrast Colors:

- Use high contrast colors for text and background to improve readability for users with low vision.

7. Provide Alternative Text for Images:

- Use the semanticLabel property of the Image widget to provide alternative text for images for screen readers.

8. Test with Accessibility Tools:

- Use accessibility tools like screen readers and accessibility scanners to test your app for accessibility issues.

9. Provide Text-to-Speech Support:

- Use the FlutterTts package to provide text-to-speech support for users with visual impairments.

10. Follow Platform Guidelines:

- Follow platform-specific accessibility guidelines, such as the Android Accessibility Guidelines and the iOS Accessibility Guidelines, to ensure your app meets platform-specific accessibility standards.

11. Conclusion:

- By following these guidelines, you can make your Flutter app more accessible to users with disabilities, providing a better user experience for all users.

Internationalization and Localization

Internationalization (i18n) and localization (l10n) are crucial for making your Flutter app accessible to users around the world. Here's how you can implement internationalization and localization in your Flutter app:

1. Internationalization (i18n):

- Internationalization is the process of designing your app to support multiple languages and regions without making changes to the source code.
- In Flutter, you can use the flutter_localizations package to add support for internationalization.
- Define your app's supported locales in the MaterialApp widget:

```dart
dart code
MaterialApp(
supportedLocales: [
const Locale('en', 'US'), // English
const Locale('es', 'ES'), // Spanish
],
localizationsDelegates: [
GlobalMaterialLocalizations.delegate,
GlobalWidgetsLocalizations.delegate,
],
localeResolutionCallback: (locale, supportedLocales) {
for (var supportedLocale in supportedLocales) {
if (supportedLocale.languageCode == locale.languageCode &&
supportedLocale.countryCode == locale.countryCode) {
return supportedLocale;
}
```

```
}
return supportedLocales.first;
},
home: MyHomePage(),
);
```

2. Localization (l10n):

- Localization is the process of adapting your app's content and user interface to different languages and regions.
- Use the intl package to add support for localization in your Flutter app.
- Define your app's localized strings in .arb files:

```
less code
{
"@@locale": "en",
"hello": "Hello, World!",
"welcome": "Welcome to my app!"
}
```

- Load the localized strings in your app using the Intl class:

```
dart code
String hello = Intl.message('hello', name: 'hello');
String welcome = Intl.message('welcome', name: 'welcome');
```

3. Pluralization and Genderization:

- Use the Intl.plural and Intl.gender methods to handle pluralization and genderization in your localized strings.

4. Date and Time Formatting:

- Use the DateFormat class to format dates and times according to the user's locale.

5. Number Formatting:

- Use the NumberFormat class to format numbers according to the user's locale.

6. Currency Formatting:

- Use the NumberFormat.currency method to format currency values according to the user's locale.

7. Testing and Verification:

- Test your app's internationalization and localization by changing the device's language and region settings.
- Use tools like flutter_l10n_gen to automate the generation of localized strings.

8. Conclusion:

- By following these guidelines, you can make your Flutter app accessible to users around the world, providing a better user experience for everyone.

Advanced Topics in Flutter

Flutter's versatility extends beyond mobile app development, offering robust solutions for web, desktop, and even embedded device applications. Here's an in-depth look at these advanced topics:

1. Flutter Web:

- Flutter Web allows you to build high-quality, interactive web applications using the same codebase as your Flutter mobile app.
- To create a Flutter web project, run the following command:

```lua
lua code
flutter create my_web_app
```

- You can then build and run your Flutter web app using:

```arduino
arduino code
flutter run -d chrome
```

- Flutter web supports most of the Flutter framework features, including stateful hot reload, widget-based UI, and platform-aware layouts.

2. Flutter for Desktop (Windows, macOS, Linux):

- Flutter for Desktop enables you to create cross-platform desktop applications for Windows, macOS, and Linux using the Flutter framework.
- To enable Flutter desktop support, run the following commands:

lua code
flutter channel dev
flutter upgrade
flutter config—enable-windows-desktop
flutter config—enable-macos-desktop
flutter config—enable-linux-desktop

- You can then create a new Flutter desktop project using:

lua code
flutter create my_desktop_app

- Flutter for Desktop provides access to native features and APIs, allowing you to create desktop applications with a native look and feel.

3. Flutter for Embedded Devices (Raspberry Pi, IoT):

- Flutter for Embedded Devices extends Flutter's capabilities to the realm of embedded systems, such as Raspberry Pi and IoT devices.
- To set up Flutter for Embedded Devices, you'll need to cross-compile the Flutter engine for your target platform.
- Flutter's architecture allows it to run efficiently on resource-constrained devices, making it suitable for a wide range of embedded applications.

4. Conclusion:

- Flutter's support for web, desktop, and embedded devices expands its potential beyond mobile app development, offering a unified framework for building applications across various platforms. By leveraging Flutter's versatility, developers can create innovative and engaging experiences for users across different devices and platforms.

Conclusion

In concluding your Flutter journey, it's important to recap key concepts, outline next steps, and provide resources for further learning.

1. Recap of Key Concepts:

- Recap the fundamental concepts covered in this book, such as widgets, state management, navigation, and internationalization.
- Highlight key takeaways and best practices for building Flutter apps.

2. Next Steps in Your Flutter Journey:

- Encourage readers to continue exploring Flutter by building more complex apps and experimenting with advanced features.
- Suggest joining the Flutter community for support and networking opportunities.
- Recommend exploring Flutter's ecosystem of packages and plugins to enhance app functionality.

3. Resources for Further Learning:

- Provide a list of recommended resources, such as books, tutorials, documentation, and online courses, for readers to deepen their Flutter knowledge.
- Mention Flutter's official website, Flutter Dev YouTube channel, and Flutter community forums as valuable resources

for learning and staying updated.

4. Conclusion:

- Conclude with a motivating message, encouraging readers to continue learning and growing as Flutter developers.
- Thank readers for embarking on this Flutter journey and express confidence in their ability to build amazing Flutter apps.

By providing a comprehensive conclusion, you can inspire readers to continue their Flutter journey with confidence and enthusiasm.

Recap of Key Concepts

Throughout this book, you've explored a wide range of key concepts in Flutter, empowering you to build beautiful and functional mobile, web, and desktop applications. Let's recap some of the key concepts you've learned:

1. Widgets:

- Widgets are the building blocks of Flutter UI, representing everything from structural elements like Container and Row to interactive components like Button and TextField.

2. State Management:

- Flutter provides various approaches to managing state, including setState for simple apps, Provider for scalable state management, and Bloc for reactive programming.

3. Navigation:

- Flutter offers flexible navigation options, such as Navigator for managing a stack of routes and PageRoute for custom transitions between screens.

4. Internationalization (i18n) and Localization (l10n):

- Flutter supports internationalization and localization, allowing you to create apps that can be easily translated into different languages and adapted to different regions.

5. Accessibility:

- Flutter provides tools and widgets for creating accessible apps, ensuring that users with disabilities can navigate and interact with your app effectively.

6. Theming and Styling:

- Flutter's theming and styling features allow you to customize the look and feel of your app, including colors, typography, and shape.

7. Advanced Topics:

- You've explored advanced topics like Flutter for web, desktop, and embedded devices, expanding your app development capabilities beyond mobile platforms.

8. Performance Optimization:

- You've learned strategies for optimizing the performance of your Flutter apps, including reducing widget rebuilds, minimizing widget size, and using performance profiling tools.

9. Deployment:

- You've gained insights into deploying Flutter apps to various platforms, including Google Play Store, Apple App Store, and web servers.

10. Continued Learning:

- Building on these concepts, there's always more to learn and explore in the world of Flutter. Keep experimenting, building, and growing as a Flutter developer.

By mastering these key concepts, you're well-equipped to create high-quality Flutter apps that delight users and make a positive impact. Keep honing your skills, exploring new possibilities, and pushing the boundaries of what's possible with Flutter.

Next Steps in Your Flutter Journey

Congratulations on completing this book and gaining a solid foundation in Flutter development! As you continue your Flutter journey, here are some next steps to further enhance your skills and expertise:

1. Build Real-World Projects:

- Apply your knowledge to real-world projects. Start with simple apps and gradually work on more complex projects to improve your skills.

2. Explore Advanced Topics:

- Dive deeper into advanced Flutter topics such as state management, animations, custom painting, and platform-specific integrations to expand your Flutter knowledge.

3. Contribute to Open Source:

- Contribute to the Flutter framework or other Flutter-related open-source projects to gain hands-on experience and give back to the community.

4. Stay Updated:

- Follow Flutter's official blog, join Flutter community forums, and attend Flutter events and meetups to stay updated on the latest trends and developments in the Flutter ecosystem.

5. Experiment with Packages:

- Explore Flutter packages on pub.dev to discover useful packages for adding new features and functionality to your apps.

6. Build a Portfolio:

- Showcase your Flutter projects on GitHub or a personal website to demonstrate your skills to potential employers or clients.

7. Join Flutter Communities:

- Join Flutter communities on social media platforms like Twitter, Reddit, and Discord to connect with other Flutter developers, ask questions, and share your knowledge.

8. Learn Dart:

- Deepen your understanding of Dart, the programming language used in Flutter, to write more efficient and effective Flutter code.

9. Take Courses and Workshops:

- Enroll in advanced Flutter courses or workshops to learn from experts and gain new insights into Flutter development.

10. Never Stop Learning:

- The world of technology is constantly evolving. Keep learning, experimenting, and pushing yourself to become a better Flutter developer.

As you embark on the next phase of your Flutter journey, remember that learning is a continuous process. Stay curious, stay passionate, and keep building amazing Flutter apps!

Resources for Further Learning

To continue your learning journey and deepen your understanding of Flutter, here are some recommended resources:

1. Flutter Documentation:

- The official Flutter documentation is an invaluable resource for learning about Flutter's features, widgets, and best practices.
- Website: Flutter Documentation

2. Flutter YouTube Channel:

- The Flutter YouTube channel features tutorials, live streams, and updates from the Flutter team.
- Channel: Flutter YouTube Channel

3. Flutter Samples GitHub Repository:

- The Flutter Samples GitHub repository contains a collection of sample Flutter apps demonstrating various features and techniques.
- Repository: Flutter Samples

4. Flutter Community:

- Join the Flutter community on platforms like Twitter, Reddit, and Discord to connect with other Flutter developers, ask questions, and share your knowledge.
- Twitter: @FlutterDev

- Reddit: r/FlutterDev
- Discord: Flutter Community Discord

5. Online Courses:

- Take online courses on platforms like Udemy, Coursera, and LinkedIn Learning to deepen your Flutter knowledge and skills.
- Courses: Udemy, Coursera, LinkedIn Learning

6. Books:

- Explore books on Flutter development for in-depth insights and tutorials on building Flutter apps.
- Books: Flutter Books

7. Flutter DevTools:

- Use Flutter DevTools to debug and profile your Flutter apps, analyze performance, and optimize your code.
- Website: Flutter DevTools

8. Flutter Create Challenge:

- Participate in the Flutter Create challenge to showcase your creativity and build innovative Flutter apps in limited code size.
- Challenge: Flutter Create Challenge

9. Flutter Packages:

- Explore the wide range of Flutter packages available on pub.dev to add new features and functionality to your Flutter apps.

- Website: pub.dev[1]

10. Flutter Engage:

- Attend Flutter Engage, Google's flagship Flutter event, to learn about the latest Flutter updates, announcements, and best practices.
- Website: Flutter Engage

These resources will help you continue your Flutter learning journey, stay updated on the latest Flutter developments, and connect with the Flutter community. Happy coding!

---

1. https://pub.dev/

Flutter Cheat Sheet

Useful Flutter Libraries and Packages

Here is a list of some useful Flutter libraries and packages that can help you enhance your Flutter app development:

1. Provider: A state management library that provides a way to manage app state without using setState.

2. GetX: A powerful library for state management, dependency injection, and routing.

3. Dio: A powerful HTTP client for making network requests in Flutter apps.

4. Shared Preferences: A plugin for reading and writing key-value pairs to persistent storage.

5. Firebase Core: The core Firebase SDK for Flutter, providing Firebase Analytics support.

6. Firebase Auth: Firebase authentication plugin, allowing users to sign in with various methods.

7. Firebase Firestore: A Flutter plugin to use Cloud Firestore, a flexible, scalable database for mobile, web, and server development from Firebase and Google Cloud.

8. Flutter Local Notifications: A plugin for displaying local notifications in Flutter apps.

9. Flutter Secure Storage: A plugin for securely storing sensitive data on the device.

10. Flutter Image Picker: A plugin for picking images from the image library or camera.

11. Flutter WebView: A plugin for displaying web content in a Flutter app.

12. Flutter PDF Viewer: A plugin for displaying PDF documents in a Flutter app.

13. Flutter SQLite: A plugin for using SQLite databases in Flutter apps.

14. Flutter Form Validation: A package for validating forms in Flutter apps.

15. Flutter Animations: A package for creating animations in Flutter apps.

These are just a few examples of the many libraries and packages available for Flutter development. You can explore more packages on pub.dev[1], the official package repository for Flutter.

---

1.   https://pub.dev/

Glossary of Terms

Here's a glossary of terms commonly used in Flutter development:

1. **Widget:** A widget is a UI element in Flutter, such as a button, text field, or container. Widgets can be combined to create complex UIs.

2. **State:** State refers to the data that can change in a Flutter app. Widgets can have either stateless or stateful behavior.

3. **Stateful Widget:** A stateful widget is a widget that can maintain state and update its appearance in response to user interactions or changes in data.

4. **Stateless Widget:** A stateless widget is a widget that does not maintain any state and does not change its appearance once it has been built.

5. **Build Method:** The build method is a required method in Flutter widgets that is responsible for building and returning the widget's UI.

6. **Hot Reload:** Hot reload is a feature in Flutter that allows you to quickly see the effects of code changes in your app without having to restart the app.

7. **MaterialApp:** MaterialApp is a widget in Flutter that configures the top-level navigation behavior and theme of the app.

8. **Scaffold:** Scaffold is a widget in Flutter that provides a framework for implementing the basic material design layout structure of an app, including app bars, drawers, and floating action buttons.

9. **MaterialApp:** MaterialApp is a widget in Flutter that configures the top-level navigation behavior and theme of the app.

10. Widget Tree: The widget tree is a hierarchical structure of widgets that defines the UI of a Flutter app. Each widget in the tree represents a part of the UI.

11. Layout Widget: Layout widgets in Flutter are used to arrange other widgets on the screen, such as rows, columns, and grids.

12. StatelessWidget: StatelessWidget is a base class for widgets that do not require mutable state.

13. StatefulWidget: StatefulWidget is a base class for widgets that require mutable state.

14. ThemeData: ThemeData is a class in Flutter that defines the visual properties, such as colors and typography, of a material design theme.

15. MediaQuery: MediaQuery is a class in Flutter that provides information about the current app's UI, such as screen size and orientation.

These are just a few of the many terms you may encounter when working with Flutter. familiarizing yourself with these terms will help you understand Flutter documentation and tutorials more effectively.

Preface

Welcome to the world of Flutter! Whether you're new to app development or a seasoned pro, this book is your guide to mastering Flutter and creating stunning native mobile, web, and desktop apps with ease.

Flutter's reactive framework and extensive widget library make it a powerful tool for building beautiful, fast apps. In this book, we'll start with the basics and progress to more advanced topics like state management, navigation, and working with APIs. You'll learn how to create custom UIs, handle user input, and integrate Firebase for backend services.

Throughout the book, we'll provide practical examples and tips to help you understand Flutter's core concepts and best practices. By the end, you'll have the skills and confidence to create high-quality Flutter apps that stand out in the app stores.

Whether you're a beginner or an experienced developer, this book will help you unlock the full potential of Flutter. Let's dive in and start building amazing apps together!

About The Author

Francis Mukobi Francis Mukobi is a passionate software developer with a deep love for creating innovative solutions using technology. With years of experience in the industry, Francis has honed his skills in mobile and web application development, specializing in Flutter, JavaScript, and other modern technologies.

Known for his attention to detail and creative approach to problem-solving, Francis has a track record of delivering high-quality projects that exceed client expectations. He is also a dedicated mentor, sharing his knowledge and expertise with aspiring developers to help them succeed in the tech industry.

In addition to his technical skills, Francis is a strong advocate for diversity and inclusion in the tech community, actively promoting opportunities for underrepresented groups. His commitment to excellence and his passion for technology make him a valuable asset to any project or team.

Books By This Author
Mastering JavaScript: Your Ultimate Guide

Welcome to "Mastering JavaScript: Your Ultimate Guide." This book is your comprehensive road-map to mastering the JavaScript programming language.

JavaScript is the cornerstone of modern web development, powering everything from interactive websites to complex web applications. In this book, we'll explore JavaScript from the ground up, covering essential concepts, advanced features, and best practices.

Throughout the book, you'll learn by doing, with hands-on exercises and real-world examples. By the end, you'll have the skills and confidence to tackle any JavaScript project with ease.

Let's dive in and master JavaScript together!

CODECRAFT: A BEGINNER'S Guide To HTML

Learn web development from scratch with our comprehensive guide! In 'CodeCraft: A Beginner's Guide To HTML,' you'll discover the fundamentals of HTML, understand how tags work, and create your own web pages. Whether you're a total beginner or need a refresher, this book equips you with the skills to build your own websites. Dive into the world of HTML and unleash your creativity!"

CodeCraft: A Beginner's Guide To CSS

You might wonder why yet another book on CSS. After all, there are countless resources out there. But let me share my perspective. As a web developer with years of experience, I've witnessed the magic that CSS brings to life. It's not just about styling web pages; it's about creating digital experiences that captivate, inform, and inspire.

This book is for you, the curious beginner who wants to build webpages from scratch. Whether you're a student, a hobbyist, or someone transitioning into tech, I've crafted this guide with your needs in mind. We'll start with the basics and gradually dive deeper, demystifying CSS properties, selectors, and layout techniques.

Don't miss out!

Visit the website below and you can sign up to receive emails whenever Francis Mukobi publishes a new book. There's no charge and no obligation.

https://books2read.com/r/B-A-QUVEB-AKKZC

BOOKS 2 READ

Connecting independent readers to independent writers.

www.ingramcontent.com/pod-product-compliance
Lightning Source LLC
Chambersburg PA
CBHW031409150726

47989CB00002B/582